ARCHITECTU:
as a Synthesis of the Arts

Eight lectures given in Berlin and Dornach
between 12 December 1911 and 26 July 1914
with an appendix featuring notes of lectures
in Munich and Stuttgart on 7 and 30 March 1914,
extracts from lectures in Dornach
on 31 December 1923 and 1 January 1924
and two newspaper articles

RUDOLF STEINER

Translated by Johanna Collis, Dorothy Osmond, Rex Raab and
Jean Schmid-Bailey

English translation edited with an
Introduction by Christian Thal-Jantzen

RUDOLF STEINER PRESS
LONDON

Rudolf Steiner Press
51 Queen Caroline Street
London W6 9QL

First published 1999

The lecture of 12 December 1911 was previously published in English under the title *And the Temple Becomes Man*, Rudolf Steiner Press 1979. The five lectures in Part Two were previously published as *Ways to a New Style in Architecture*, Anthroposophical Publishing Co., London and Anthroposophic Press, New York, 1927

Originally published in German under the title *Wege zu einem neuen Baustil*, *'Und der Bau wird Mensch'*, volume 286 in the Rudolf Steiner *Gesamtausgabe* or collected works, by Rudolf Steiner Verlag, Dornach, Switzerland. This authorized translation is based on the third edition and published by kind permission of the Rudolf Steiner Nachlassverwaltung, Dornach

Translation © Rudolf Steiner Press 1999

A catalogue record for this book is available from the British Library

The publishers gratefully acknowledge the sponsorship and cooperation in the publication of this volume by the Art Section of the School of Spiritual Science, Dornach

ISBN 1 85584 057 X

Cover by Trisha Connolly, incorporating artwork by Anne Stockton
Typeset by DP Photosetting, Aylesbury, Bucks
Printed and bound in Great Britain by Cromwell Press Limited, Trowbridge, Wiltshire

Contents

CREDITS

PLATES:
Pastel drawings by Wilfred Norton reproduced by kind permission from the
private collections of the following: Plate 2, Christian Thal-Jantzen; Plates 3,
5, John Wilkes; Plate 4, Edith Bierman
Photos on Plates 6, 7, 8 by Thorwald Thiersch

ILLUSTRATIONS WITHIN TEXT:
Pages vi, 6, 7, 28, 29, 36, 37, 42, 44, 49, 154, 169, 176: photos by Christian Thal-
Jantzen
Pages 33, 34, 77, 98: photos by O. Rietmann
Pages 36, 42, 44, 45, 47, 48, 55, 79 (above), 159, 174: drawings by Hansjörg Palm
Pages 38, 79 (below): drawings by Erich Zimmer
Pages 58, 59, 61, 62 (below), 88, 92, 93, 99, 102, 103, 105 (above), 106 (above),
107 (above), 108 (left), 112 (left), 113 (left), 121: drawn during lecture by
Louise Boesé
Page 68: Townley Collection, British Museum, London
Pages 69, 90, 105 (below), 106 (below), 107 (below), 108 (right), 112 (right),
113 (right): drawings by Meta Waller Pyle
Pages 83, 86: drawn during lecture by Louise Clason
Pages 96, 97, 168: drawings by Yugi Agematsu and Rex Raab
Pages 118, 119, 120: drawn during lecture by Beate Meyer Jacobs
Page 161: drawings by Johanna Berger
Pages xiv, xv, 165: photos by Thorwald Thiersch
Page 171: drawing by Hermann Ranzenberger

Second Goetheanum. Auditorium base of Mars pillar executed 1997
under the direction of Christian Hitsch, based on designs of Rudolf Steiner

Introduction

It is hard to appreciate the significance of Rudolf Steiner as an artist and architect if one has not stood before the west front of the present Goetheanum. The illustrations in this book give an indication of that unique building as well as its predecessor on the same site, known as the First Goetheanum. The present building was begun in 1924 and has been gradually completed up to the present day. The first building was begun in 1913 and destroyed, by suspected arson, in 1922. Steiner was responsible for the design of a further 17 buildings, constructed between 1908 and 1924, 14 of which survive today in the vicinity of the Second Goetheanum in Dornach, near Basle, Switzerland. His main purpose was to create a synthesis of the visual arts, within an architectural setting, which revealed spiritual realities usually hidden from everyday consciousness. This required the participation of the arts of painting, sculpture and coloured glass engraving.

Steiner was also interested in exploring how the medium of the visual arts can convey the results of spiritual-scientific research in a manner not possible through the use of words. In the case of painting, his own work began in 1916 with his sketches for 26 paintings that were to cover the inside of the large and the small cupola of the First Goetheanum. Seven of these were executed by him personally. His sketches for the large cupola have recently been used as the basis for the ceiling paintings in the auditorium of the Second Goetheanum (parts of this ceiling can be seen in Plates 6–8). Steiner went on to advise on the training of painters, producing numerous paintings and sketches as training exercises.

His work on the potential of coloured glass engraving began in 1915 with his sketches for the 24 coloured glass engraved windows for the auditorium of the First Goetheanum and the three windows for the west entrance lobby. The quite extraordinary coloured lighting effect can be seen in the coloured illustrations. Assja Turgenieff worked out the designs in collaboration with Rudolf Steiner during the early nineteen-twenties. The coloured windows in the Second Goetheanum are based on this work and were completed by Assja Turgenieff in 1928 (two of these windows can be seen in Plate 7). The English artist Wilfred Norton captured the magical effect of the light falling through the coloured glass and playing on the sculptural forms. He is the only person to have made interior studies of the First Goetheanum. (Some of Norton's drawings are reproduced, for the first time, in Plates 2–5.)

Steiner's collaboration with the English sculptress, Edith Maryon, enabled him to explore the art of sculpture. The First Goetheanum was carved and modelled inside and out, introducing dynamic movement and form on a monumental scale. The carved portals, capitals, bases and architraves of the auditorium and stage of the First Goetheanum were all based on his designs. They are outstanding examples of an art form that is both architecture and sculpture. This was to be taken further on a grand scale in the exterior of the Second Goetheanum. Steiner's major free-standing figurative sculptural work is known as The Representative of Man. This wooden sculpture was intended for the east end of the stage of the First Goetheanum. Fortunately it survived the burning of the First Goetheanum and is now exhibited in the south wing of the Second Goetheanum.

Apart from his work as a visual artist, Steiner was a phenomenal lecturer. From 1902 to 1924 he gave over 6,000 lectures, and wrote 28 books. The lectures and articles in this book provide a small but significant selection for anyone who has an interest in and love for the visual arts in their fullest sense—arts that can move the human soul, arts that can reveal the innermost secrets of the universe, arts that can awaken us to our highest aspirations, to our sense of divine origins and to responsibility for our actions.

*   *   *

With the exception of the two articles in the Appendix, all the material in this book was delivered to an audience assumed by Steiner to be familiar with the basic ideas of anthroposophical spiritual science. Readers who have not previously come across his philosophy might find this assumed familiarity a handicap, but I would ask them to be patient. Publishing the material in the form of lecture notes is, in a sense, a compromise. The ideal would have been for Steiner to be have been able to publish his results in a written book. This was his intention. In the event he was not even able to check the notes taken during his lectures. One advantage of this is that the texts have directness and give a flavour of the mood of the time as experienced by his listeners. There is a strong sense of purpose and mission running through all the lectures, such as his concern that the visual arts should transform our consciousness and help build a vibrant new social order.

Rudolf Steiner's work as a visual artist and architect is both unique and a child of its time. The contents of this book aim to give evidence of that unique contribution to the visual arts. There were numerous outstanding architects in the second half of the nineteenth century who have in common with each other and with Steiner a complete break with tradition and conventionality. For example Antonio Gaudi (1852–1926) 'was one of those overwhelming personalities like Francesco Borromini or William Blake who appeared to break free from the frame of their cultural context'.[1] Or take Victor Horta (1861–1947), who in an age of historicism and eclecticism refused point-blank to participate. 'I have no right to copy the forms reflecting the character or the people who invented them. I do have a right to create!' Horta did create a new and dynamic visual language. The ground for this breakthrough by the likes of Steiner, Gaudi and Horta was laid by the Englishman William Morris (1834–1896). He refuted the then current historicism, the 'masquerading in other peoples' cast-off clothes'.[2] He envisaged a time when daily labour would be sweetened by 'the daily creation of Art' and 'a happiness for the maker and the user', so Art should be Art not only 'by the people' but also 'for the people'.

What Rudolf Steiner has in common with William Morris, Victor Horta and Antonio Gaudi is a devotion to finding the truth through art; that the appearance of an object should be truthful in the sense that it is suitable for its purpose, and at the same time beautiful; that the 'form should follow the function'. The challenge for Steiner was to meet the practical functional requirements to a degree equal with the requirement for an appropriate soul mood. The result would give rise to forms and colours that would inspire the highest spiritual aspirations of the human being. He did this engaging not only what is commonly thought of as architecture, but also the arts of painting and sculpture, seeking for a higher synthesis of all the visual arts, a kind of visual symphony.

The ideal of creating a symphonic whole of all the major visual arts within a building surrounded by a community striving to be integrated through a common architectural style was one that lived among Rudolf Steiner's contemporaries. Unlike them, however, Steiner achieved this ideal, in Dornach. As early as 1900, the well-known architect, Peter Behrens, wrote in an article, 'Festivals of Light and Art': 'At the edge of a grove on a crest of a hill shall this solemn building raise its walls. If down below in our familiar environment we had arranged everything to relate to our daily lives, to the logic of our thoughts, and to our material sense of purpose, up there we should be filled with a sense of a higher purpose, a purpose that was merely translated into material terms, a spiritual need, the gratification of our transcendental nature.' This can be experienced in Dornach today.

A further example of the vision for an integrated art and architecture as a force for social revolution is set out in 1918 in the architectural programme of the *Arbeitsrat* (Works Council): '... there will be no boundaries between the crafts, sculpture, and painting, all will be one: architecture. A building is the direct carrier of spiritual values, shaper of the sensibilities of the general public, which slumber today but will awake tomorrow. Only a total revolution in the realm of the spiritual will create this building; yet this revolution, this building, does not happen by itself. Both have to be sought—today's architects must prepare the way for this edifice.'

The third lecture of Part I of this book illustrates Rudolf Steiner's vision to create an architecturally coherent and integrated community around the Goetheanum, and the envisaged impact of the artistic unity on the social coherence and harmony of the community. In the second lecture of Part II you will find clearly spelt out how Steiner saw that architecture has the potential for preventing criminality and supporting a law abiding society in a way that actual laws can never do. He was entirely in harmony and sympathy with his contemporaries on these issues. Where he differed was that he actually managed to realize his vision, which can be viewed today in Dornach.

*   *   *

The first lecture in Part I was given at the inaugural meeting of the association founded to promote the building that was later to become the First Goetheanum. At the time of the lecture that building was planned for Munich in Southern Germany. The second lecture was given to the same body just over a year later. In both these lectures Steiner spoke about the origin of architecture within the human soul and traced the parallel development of sacred and temple architecture with the evolution of the human soul.

In May 1913 the decision was announced that the building projected for Munich was to be erected instead at Dornach near Basle in Switzerland. The model and illustrations of the new project for Dornach were presented to a general meeting of the Anthroposophical Society in Berlin in January 1914; it was also at that general meeting that a working party of artists was appointed. The idea of a community of private residences, as well as workshops, laboratories and offices surrounding the main building, had been part of the Munich project and was developed further in Dornach. On 23 January 1914 Rudolf Steiner addressed the Building Association, sharing his vision of how an integrated visual architectural community might be created. This forms the third lecture in Part I.

The five lectures in Part II were all given in Dornach to an audience largely made up of Rudolf Steiner's fellow artists and others working on the construction of the Goetheanum. The lectures were given in the temporary carpentry workshop erected adjacent to the construction site. Contemporary reports describe how the workshop was converted into a lecture hall at the end of the working day. One of these reports is by the artist Natalie Turgenieff-Pozzo: 'A small space in the carpentry workshop was cleared of shavings and planks to accommodate chairs for the elderly members. The rest of us sat on the workbenches, on crates and stacked planks, or simply on the floor. We enjoyed the unaccustomed surroundings with the white wooden planks setting off people's bright clothes. Dr Steiner entered and looked around; he was never indifferent to his surroundings. He saw the various colour combinations, regarded the way people were grouped and nodded his greeting in all directions; he noticed everything and was amused by his auditorium. These lectures were cheerful courses of instruction, bright and lively. At a distance he was still often taken for a young man. The summer was exceptionally hot but nevertheless the work was hastened along.'[3]

*   *   *

Art was firmly on Steiner's agenda from Whitsun 1907 onwards. On that occasion he organized the artistic display at a congress of the Theosophical Society in Munich[4]. The programme for this congress included a play, poetry readings and music, all in a dramatic architectural setting of bright red draped walls with seven large paintings illustrating the Apocalypse, and seven painted columns. The capitals on these columns anticipate the sevenfold metamorphosis that was to reappear in subsequent building designs, including Malsch 1909, Stuttgart 1911, Munich 1911 to 1913 and Dornach 1913.

In 1908 an artistic centre was opened to the public in Munich. In the summer of 1909 a production of Edouard Schuré's mystery play took place there and in the following four years productions were mounted of each of Rudolf Steiner's four mystery plays. The dramatic art form was explored as a vehicle for conveying the true nature of the incarnated human being as revealed by spiritual-scientific research. It was realized that a purpose-built theatre was needed for this work. Steiner's own words describe this process best:

It was my belief that I had to direct all my energies towards the cultivation of the inner, spiritual work of anthroposophy, and I was grateful for the initiative taken to create a home for this work. When the initiative was about to become a reality, the artistic design of the building became for me a matter of this inner, spiritual work, and this became my task. I asserted that the artistic forms must proceed on the same principles as those from which anthroposophical thought itself issues if the building is to be a true home for anthroposophy. That the design must not be insipidly allegorical or make use of sickly symbolism lies in the very essence of anthroposophy, which I am convinced leads of itself to true art.

The plan to execute the building in Munich could not be realized because established artistic circles objected to the forms that it was to be given. Whether or not these objections might have been overcome later is no longer relevant. The representatives of the Building Association wanted construction to proceed without delay and therefore gratefully accepted the gift of a plot of land from Dr Emil Grosheintz, which he had previously acquired on the Dornach Hill. Thus it became possible to lay the foundation stone on 20 September 1913 and proceed immediately with the construction.

Those in charge of the project called the building 'Johannesbau' after Johannes Thomasius, a character in my mystery dramas. During the years when the building was under construction I often mentioned that when I began cultivating anthroposophical thought many years ago I had proceeded from a study of Goethe and that for me the home of anthroposophy would be called a Goetheanum. Thereupon pre-eminently non-German members of the Anthroposophical Society resolved to call the building The Goetheanum in the future.

At the time of the building's construction anthroposophy had already gained members who had been trained and had worked in the most diverse fields of science, and the prospect thus existed of applying the methods of spiritual science within the other sciences. I therefore venture to suggest adding to the name of the building the designation 'School of Spiritual Science'.[5]

These words were written in January 1923 immediately following the destruction by fire of the First Goetheanum on the night of 31 December 1922. This event was an enormous blow—physically, emotionally and spiritually to Rudolf Steiner and his fellow artists. Thousands of hours of work had gone up in flames in a single night. The health of his close collaborator Edith Maryon collapsed and she never recovered, dying just over a year later. Although deeply affected, Steiner determined to continue the work, and he set about preparation for a replacement building. A year later to the day, he presented his initial ideas for the new design in two talks, which are included in the Appendix of this volume.

The first two items in the Appendix are fragments in which Steiner drew attention to the importance of architectural building initiatives, particularly at the turn of every millennium. He described the condition of the western human soul at each millennium beginning with 3,000 BC through to the imminent year AD 2,000. The Goetheanum building now standing on the hill at Dornach is intended as a contribution towards the opposing of destructive forces being unleashed within the human soul as the new millennium approaches.

* * *

When the Second Goetheanum was opened in 1928 it was still largely an outer shell, unfinished inside. Rudolf Steiner had not had the opportunity to prepare detailed designs for the interior before his untimely death in March 1925. It has therefore fallen to others to complete the present Goetheanum, inspired no doubt by Steiner's words reproduced in this book and elsewhere.

The major steps in this completion were the responsibility of the following. 1925: the enlarging of Steiner's exterior model to the full size—Albert Dubach and Carl Kemper, sculptors; 1928: the coloured glass engraved windows—Assja Turgenieff, artist; 1930: the interior of the south entrance and staircase—Carl Kemper, sculptor; 1935: exhibition space for the wooden sculpture—Meta Waller Pyle and Otto Moser; 1957: auditorium—Johannes Schöpfer, architect; 1964: the west entrance area, west staircase and cloakrooms—Rex Raab, architect and Arne Klingborg, artist; west doors—Rex Raab, John Wilkes, artist; 1971: the English Hall—Rex Raab, architect—Gerard Wagner, painter; 1984: Ticket Hall—Portus Bau, Fritz Marburg, sculptor and Wilfried Reindel, architect; 1987: the north wing, mainly Mathias Ganz, architect; 1993: the external works of roadways, paths, benches, lamps and planting—Marianne Schubert, landscape architect, and Hansjörg Palm, sculptor/designer; 1997: remodelling of auditor-

Second Goetheanum. Main entrance to building with lamp designed by Hansjörg Palm 1993

ium—artistic conception Christian Hitsch, artist, and Ulrich Oelssner, architect.

The most recent stage has been the remodelling of the auditorium which now has 'living walls' as described by Steiner in Part II, Lecture 2, with a flowing 'sea of colour' overhead on the ceiling, as described in Part II, Lecture 5. Christian Hitsch is the artist responsible for the artistic conception of this design. He has worked with the same underlying idea of sevenfold metamorphosis as can be found in Steiner's designs for the Munich Congress 1907, Malsch 1909, Stuttgart 1911, Munich 1911 to 1913 and in the First Goetheanum, Dornach 1913. For the ceiling painting, the sketches prepared by Steiner for the Great Hall of the First Goetheanum likewise underlie the approach to the new ceiling, albeit now in a very different configuration. As in his day, this latest stage of the work has been a team effort with many artists and craftspeople from all over the world working together.

The American sculptor, Michael Howard, spent about six weeks during 1997 working on the building as a carver. He wrote in a letter to fellow artists in America: 'In that period about 30 sculptors carved most of the south wall—architraves, capitals,

Second Goetheanum. Auditorium north wall showing carved architrave and seven pillars with carved capitals and bases. Executed 1997 under the direction of Christian Hitsch, based on designs by Rudolf Steiner

pillars and base motifs. It was an exciting experience to see all the technical innovations that had been developed to make this project possible. But it was even more impressive to see how all the artists and collaborators gave of themselves. Christian Hitsch was particularly able to inspire confidence in the artists to find their individual path to the final forms in such a way that the diverse levels and types of gifts of each artist enhanced rather than detracted from the living quality of the forms.'

The English architect, Tony Cooper, visited the new Goetheanum hall as its interior was nearing completion in late 1997 and wrote:

My first impression was that I felt that space was holding me in a consciousness of active interest, an almost forgotten function in current world architecture. The interior invited me to enter into a dialogue with it and touch it with all my senses. The impression of softness of surface is quite tangible; the colour of the material is soft, the facets of the carving move softly to blend one with another; the quality of sound has an active softness and the light, even without the coloured glass windows, flows happily around and on to the forms, picking out the magical sparkle of the marble aggregate in the material. Nothing accosts the senses, there is no starkness, no angles clash and jar, nothing but a sense of exciting and enthusiastic life forces responding to human consciousness in them. Spaces and buildings are often high, often too high. Levity is a subtle and delightful expression of the activity of light, especially when the feeling of being drawn up is brought to a dynamic conclusion in a progression of evolving capital forms. These are held in the space above by a carved architrave with all the grace of a wave that has rolled through seas of evolution. A quite new architectural element in this composition is the short wall elements which hold the capital and give the windows a definitive space. They clearly soar like columns, which they are not; they have something of the pilaster, which they are not. They are much more individual and alive. They could be related to Gothic buttresses ... I cannot help feeling that they are ethereally buttressing the world forces outside the main walls; what a happy imagination! The space is amplified by these elements, not only by holding and defining the seating area but by giving a sense of contained rhythm and movement towards the stage.[6]

C.F.T-J., Hoathly Hill Community, Sussex, England
November 1998

PART I

AND THE TEMPLE IS THE HUMAN BEING

AN ART AND ARCHITECTURE THAT REVEAL THE UNDERLYING WHOLENESS OF CREATION
Complementing the modern tendency to analyse and dissect

Lecture One, Berlin, 12 December 1911[1]

The free creative activity of human beings is put to the test

In the building that is to be a home for spiritual science, full account must be taken of the evolutionary conditions and necessities of mankind as a whole. Unless this requirement is met the aim of such a building will not be achieved. In an undertaking like this we have a deep responsibility to what we know to be the laws of the spiritual life, the powers of the spiritual world and the conditions of human evolution; and above all we must be mindful of the judgement which future times will make. In the present cycle of human evolution this responsibility is altogether different from what it was in times gone by.

Great creations of art and culture have many things to tell us of bygone ages. In a beautiful and impressive lecture this morning,[2] you heard how they help us understand the inner constitution and attitude of the human soul in former times.

Those who shared in the creation of ancient works of art had less burden of responsibility than we do today, because in ancient times human beings had at their disposal means of help which are no longer available in our epoch. In those days the gods let their forces stream into the unconscious or subconscious life of human beings. So in a certain sense it is an illusion to believe that in the minds or souls of the men who built the pyramids of Egypt, the temples of Greece and other great monuments, only human thoughts were responsible for the impulses and aims expressed in the forms, the colours and so on. In those times the gods themselves were working through the hands, heads and hearts of human beings.

The fourth post-Atlantean epoch[3] now lies in the distant past and our age is the first period of time in which the gods are putting the free creative activity of human beings to the test. They do not actually withhold their help, but they vouchsafe it only when human beings out of their own individual soul, developed through a number of incarnations, freely aspire to receive the forces streaming to them from above. What we have to create is essentially new, in the sense that we must work with forces which are altogether different from those obtaining in bygone times. We have to create out of the free activity of our own human souls. The hallmark of our age is consciousness, for it is the consciousness soul which is the characteristic feature of the present epoch. If the future is to receive from us works of culture and of art such as we have received from the past, we must create out of full and clear consciousness, free from any influence arising out of our sub-conscious life. That is why we must open our minds and hearts to thoughts which shed light upon the task ahead of us. Only if we know upon what laws and fundamental spiritual impulses our work must be grounded, only if what we do is in line and in har-mony with the evolutionary forces operating in mankind as a whole, will achievement be within our reach.

A building that enshrines what is held most sacred

Let us now turn to certain basic ideas which can make our work fruitful in creating something that is fundamentally new, new in its very essence.

In a sense our intention is to build a temple that is also to be a place of teaching, as were the ancient temples of the Mysteries. Buildings erected to enshrine what human beings have held most sacred have always been known as temples. You have already heard how the life of the human soul in the different epochs came to expression in temple buildings. When we study these buildings with insight and warmth of soul, differences are at once apparent. A very striking example is given by the forms of temple belonging to the second post-Atlantean epoch of culture. Outwardly, at any rate, very little is left of these ancient Persian temples, and their original form can only be dimly pictured or reconstructed from the Akashic Record.[4] Something reminiscent of their forms did indeed find its way into the later temples of the third epoch, into

Babylonian-Assyrian architecture, and above all into the temples of Asia Minor, but only in those aspects that are typical of the region as such.

The most striking and significant feature of early architecture

Documentary records have little information to give on the subject. But if, assuming that investigation of the Akashic Record itself is not possible, we study the remains of buildings of a later epoch, gleaning from them some idea of what the earlier temples in that part of the world may have been, we shall begin to realize that in these very ancient temples everything depended on the façade, on the impression made by the front of the temple on those who approached its portals. A person making his way through this façade into the interior of the temple would have felt that the façade spoke to him in a secret, mysterious language; in the interior of the temple he found everything that was striving to express itself in the façade. He would have felt this no matter whether he came as a layman or as one who had been initiated.

Turning now from these temples—the character of which can only be dimly surmised by those unable to read the Akashic Record—to the temples of Egypt, or other sacred buildings such as the pyramids, we find something altogether different. Symbolic figures of mystery and grandeur stand before us as we approach an ancient Egyptian temple; the sphinx, the pyramids and even the obelisks are riddles—so much so that the German philosopher Hegel spoke of this art as the art of the 'enigma'.[5]

The upward-rising form of the pyramid, in which there is scarcely an aperture, seems to enshrine a mystery; the outer façade presents us with a riddle. In the interior, we find indications of something that is to lead the hearts and souls of human beings to the god who dwelt in deep concealment within the innermost sanctuary. We also find information on manifold secrets written in the ancient Mystery-script, or what later took its place. While the temple enshrines the most sacred Mystery—the Mystery of the God—pyramids in their very architecture enshrine the Mystery of the human being, of initiation, of which the inmost secrets must be hidden away from the external world.

The temples of Greece retain the basic principle of many Egyptian temples as dwelling places of the divine, spiritual pre-

The Sphinx, Giza   *Avenue of the Sphinx, Luxor Temple*

sence. But the outer structure itself indicates a further stage. In the Greek temple's wonderful expression of dynamic power, not in the forms alone but in inner forces weaving in the forms, it is whole and complete, intrinsically perfect—an infinitude in itself. The Greek god dwells within this temple. In this building, the proportions of whose columns have an inner dynamic exactly suited to the weight they are expected to support, the god is enshrined in something that is whole and perfect in itself, that depicts in every detail, from the grandest to the tiniest, an infinitude in finite earthly existence.

The idea embodied in the Christian church is the temple as an expression of all that is most precious to human beings. Such buildings, erected originally over a grave, indeed over the grave of the Redeemer, later came to adjoin a spire tapering upwards to the heights. In a church we have the expression of an altogether new impulse, whereby Christian temple architecture is distinguished from that of Greece. The Greek temple is self-sufficient, a single complete, dynamic whole. But a Christian church is quite different. I once said[6] that by its very nature, a temple dedicated to Pallas Athene, to Apollo or to Zeus needs no human being near it or inside it; it stands there in its own self-contained, solitary majesty as the dwelling-place of the god. The Greek temple is an infinitude in itself in that it is the dwelling-place of the

Parthenon, Athens

*Coutances Cathedral,
Normandy*

god, so that the further away people are from it, the truer it
appears. Paradoxical as it may seem, this is the conception
underlying the Greek temple. A Christian church is quite different. Its forms call out to the hearts and minds of the faithful. Every
detail in the space we enter tells us that it exists in order to receive
the congregation with all their thoughts, aspirations and feelings.[7]

A Gothic church, with its characteristic forms, tries to express
something that is not as separate and complete in itself as a Greek
temple. In each and every form Gothic architecture seems to reach
out beyond its own boundaries, to express the aspirations and
searchings of those within its walls; everywhere there is a kind of
urge to break through the enclosing walls and mingle with the
universe. The Gothic arch arose, of course, from a feeling for
dynamic proportion; but apart from this there is something in all
Gothic forms that seems to lead out and beyond; they strive to
make themselves permeable. One of the reasons why a Gothic
building makes its wonderful impression is that the many-coloured
windows provide such a mysterious and yet such a natural link
between the interior space and the all-pervading light. Could there
be any sight in the world more radiant and glorious than that of the
light streaming in through the stained-glass windows of a Gothic
cathedral among the dancing specks of dust? Could any enclosed
space make a more majestic impression than this—where even the

enclosing walls seem to lead out beyond themselves, where the interior space itself reaches out to the mysteries of infinite space?

The earliest temples of Asia Minor. A picture of the upright human form

This rapid survey of a lengthy period in the development of temple architecture has shown how this art develops in step with human evolution as though based on an underlying law. But for all that, we are still faced with a sphinx-like riddle. What is really at the root of it? Why has it developed in this specific way? Can any explanation be given for those remarkable fronts and façades covered with strange figures of winged animals or winged wheels, for the curious columns and capitals to be found in the region of Asia Minor as the last surviving fragments of the first stage of temple architecture? These fronts tell us something very remarkable; they tell us exactly the same, in a way, as is experienced within the temple itself. Can there be any greater enigma than the forms that are to be seen even today on fragments preserved in modern museums? What principle underlies it all?

There is an explanation, but it can only be found through insight into the thoughts and aims of those who participated in the building of these temples. This, of course, is a matter in which the help of spiritual vision is indispensable. What is a temple of Asia Minor in reality? Does its prototype or model exist anywhere in the world?

The following will indicate what this prototype is and throw light upon the whole subject. Imagine a human being lying on the ground, in the act of bringing his upper body and countenance upright. From a prostrate position the trunk is raised so that it may come within the sphere of the downstreaming spiritual forces and be united with them. This image will give you an inkling of the inspiration from which the architectural forms of the early temples of Asia Minor were born. All the columns, capitals and remarkable figures of such temples are a symbolic expression of what we may feel at the sight of a human being raising himself upright— with all that is revealed by the movements of his hands, his features, the look on his face, and so on. If with the eyes of the spirit we were able to look behind this countenance into the inner human being, into the microcosm that is an image of the macro-cosm, we should find—inasmuch as the countenance expresses the inner man—that the countenance and the inner human being are related in the same way as the façade or front of a temple of Asia Minor was related to its interior.

A human being in the act of raising himself upright is what the early temple of Asia Minor expresses, not as a copy, but as the underlying motif and all that this motif suggests. The spiritual picture given by anthroposophy of the physical nature of man helps us to realize the sense in which such a temple is an expression of the microcosm, of the human being. An understanding of the aspiring human being, therefore, sheds light on the fundamental character of that early architecture. The spiritual counterpart of the human being, as a physical being, is impressed on those remarkable temples of which only fragments and ruins have survived. This could be pointed out in every detail, down to the winged wheels and the original forms of all such designs. The temple is indeed the human being! This rings out to us across the ages like a clarion call.

The temples of Egypt and Greece. Buildings permeated by soul

So what about the temples of Egypt and Greece? The human being can be described not only as a physical being but also as a being of soul. When we approach the human being on earth as a being of soul, all that we perceive at first in his eyes, his countenance, his gestures is a riddle as great in every respect as that presented by the Egyptian temple. Within the human being we find the holy of holies, accessible only to those who can find the way from the outer to the inner. There, in the innermost sanctuary, a human soul is concealed, just as the god and the secrets of the Mysteries were concealed in the temples and pyramids of Egypt.

But the soul is not so deeply concealed in a human being as to be unable to find expression in his whole bearing and appearance. When the soul truly permeates the body, the body becomes the outward expression and manifestation of the soul. The human body is then revealed to us as a work of artistic perfection, permeated by soul, an infinitude complete in itself. Look for something in the visible world that is as whole and perfect in itself as the physical body of the human being permeated by his soul. In respect of dynamic perfection you will find nothing except the Greek temple which, in its self-contained perfection, is at the same time the dwelling-place and the expression of the god. In the sense that the human being, as microcosm, is a soul within a body, so the temple of Egypt and the temple of Greece is in reality the human being.

The human being raising himself upright is the prototype of the temple in Asia Minor. The human being standing on the earth, concealing a mysterious world within himself but able to let the forces of this inner world stream perpetually through his being, directing his gaze horizontally forward, closed in from above and below—that is the Greek temple. Again the annals of world history tell us that the temple is indeed the human being!

The mystery of Solomon's Temple. Present, yet unseen

We are now approaching our own epoch. Its origin is to be found in the fruits of the ancient Hebrew culture and of Christianity, the Mystery of Golgotha, although initially the new impulse had to find its way through architectural forms handed down from Egypt and from Greece. But the urge was to break through these forms, to break through their boundaries in such a way that they led out beyond all enclosed space to the weaving life of the universe.

The seeds of whatever happens in the future have always been sown in the past. The temple of the future is foreshadowed, mysteriously, in the past. As I am speaking of something that is a perpetual riddle in the evolution of humanity, I can hardly do otherwise than speak of the riddle itself in rather enigmatic terms.

Reference is often made to Solomon's Temple.[8] We know that it was meant to be an expression of the spiritual realities of human evolution. The enigma is that it is pointless to ask who has ever seen this Temple of Solomon about which such grand truths are uttered. Herodotus travelled in Egypt and the region of Asia Minor only a few centuries after the Temple of Solomon must have been built.[9] From his account of his travels—which mentions matters of far less importance—we know that he must have passed within a few miles of Solomon's Temple, but did not set eyes on it. People had not yet seen this temple.

The enigma is that something certainly existed and yet had not been seen. But so it is. In nature, too, there is something that may be present and yet not seen. The comparison is not perfect, however, and to press it any further would lead wide of the mark. Plants are contained within their seeds, but human eyes do not see the plants within the seeds. This comparison, as I said, must not be pressed any further; for anyone attempting to base an explanation of Solomon's Temple upon it would immediately be saying something incorrect. In the way I have expressed it, however, the comparison between the seed of a plant and the Temple of Solomon is correct.

What is the aim of Solomon's Temple? Its aim is the same as that of the temple of the future.

The physical human being can be described by anthroposophy; the human being as the temple of the soul can be described by psychosophy; and as spirit, the human being can be described by pneumatosophy.[10] Can we not, then, picture man spiritually as a human being lying on the ground and raising himself upright; then standing before us as a self-contained whole, a self-grounded, independent infinitude, with eyes gazing straight ahead; and finally as a human being whose gaze is directed to the heights, who raises his soul to the spirit which he is receiving. To say that the spirit is spiritual is tautology, but for all that it underlines what is meant, namely, that the spirit is a supersensible reality. Art, however, can work and be expressed only in the realm of the senses. In other words, the spirit that is received into the soul must be able to pour itself into form. Just as the human being raising himself upright, and then consolidated in himself, were prototypes of the ancient temples, so the prototype of the temple of the future must be the human soul into which the spirit is being received. The mission of our age is to found an architecture which will be able to say with clarity to people of the future that the temple is indeed the human being receiving the spirit into his soul.

The new temple. The incarnate spirit revealed

This new temple architecture will differ from all its predecessors, and this brings us back to what was said at the beginning of the lecture. With our physical eyes we can actually see a human being in the act of raising himself upright. But one whose being is suffused by soul must be inwardly felt, inwardly perceived. Merely looking is not enough. As you heard this morning, the sight of a Greek temple 'makes us aware in the very marrow of our bones'. Truly, the Greek temple lives within us because we are that temple, in so far as each of us is a microcosm permeated by soul. The quickening of the soul by the spirit is an invisible, supersensible fact, and yet it must become perceptible in the world of the senses if it is to be expressed in art.

No epoch except our own, and the one to come, could give birth to this form of art. Today we have to make a beginning, although it can be no more than that, an attempt—rather as when the temple which, having previously been whole and perfect in itself, strove in Christian churches to break through its own walls and make connection with the weaving life of the universe.

What do we need to build?

We need to build something which will bring to a culmination what has just been described. With the powers that spiritual science can awaken in each of us we must try to create an interior space which, in the effects produced by its colours, forms and other features, is a place set apart; but not shut off, for wherever we look our eyes and our hearts should be invited to penetrate through the walls. So that while secluded, as though within a sanctuary, we are at the same time at one with the weaving life of the divine. The temple that belongs truly to the future will have walls—and yet no walls. Its interior will have renounced every trace of egoism that may be associated with an enclosed space, and all its colours and forms will give expression to a selfless endeavour to receive the inpouring forces of the universe. At the inauguration of our building in Stuttgart[11] I tried to indicate what can be achieved in this direction by colours and how colours can be the link with the spirits of the environment present in the spiritual atmosphere.

Where is the supersensible aspect of the human being revealed to us within the physical body? Only when he speaks, when he pours his inner life of soul into the word; when the word is the embodiment of wisdom and prayer, entrusting itself to the human being as it enshrines world-mysteries. The word that becomes flesh within the human being is the spirit expressing itself in the physical body. We shall either create the building we ought to create, or we shall fail. If we fail, the task will have to be left to those who come after us. But we shall have succeeded if, for the first time, we give the interior space the most perfect form that is possible today, no matter what the outside appearance of the building may be. The exterior may or may not be prosaic; basically that is of no consequence. The outside appearance is there for the secular world which is not concerned with the interior. It is the interior that is of importance, so what will it be like?

The interior. A union of form and content

At every turn our eyes will light upon something that says to us: This interior, with its language of colours and forms, in its whole living reality, is an expression of the word spoken in this place, that most spiritual element which the human being can enshrine within his physical body. The word that reveals the riddle of the human being in wisdom and in prayer will be at one, in this building, with the forms that surround the interior space. The words sent forth into this space will set their own range and boundaries, so that as they come up against the walls they will find something to which they are so attuned that what has issued from the human being will resound back into the space again. The dynamic power of the word will go forth from the centre to the periphery, and the interior space itself will then re-echo the proclamation and message of the spirit. This interior will be enclosed and yet open to infinitudes of spirit—though not by means of windows, but by its very shape and form.

Such a building could not have existed before, for spiritual science alone is capable of creating it, and it must create such a building at some time. If it does not do this in our day, future epochs will compel it to. Just as the temple of Asia Minor, the temple of Egypt, the temple of Greece, the church or cathedral of Christianity has arisen in the course of the evolution of humanity, so must the place of the mysteries of spiritual science—secluded from the affairs of the material world and open to the spiritual world—be born from the spirit of the human being as the work of art of the future. Nothing that is already in existence can pre-figure the ideal structure that ought, one day, to stand before us. Everything about it must be new. Naturally, it will arise in a form

Bird's-eye view of Munich project, 1911

Model of Munich project, 1911

as yet imperfect, but at least it will be a beginning, leading to higher and higher degrees of perfection in this domain.

A modern building for modern times

How can modern people become mature enough to understand the nature of such a building?

No true art can arise unless it is born from the all-pervading spirit of an epoch of human evolution. During the second year of my studies at the technical university in Vienna, Ferstel,[12] the architect of the *Votivkirche* there, said something in his rectorial address that often comes back to me. On the one hand his words seemed to me at the time to strike a discordant note, but on the other they were absolutely characteristic of the times. He made the remarkable statement that architectural styles are not invented—to which we would have to add that by implication they are born from the intrinsic character of nations. Up to now, our own age has not shown the same aptitude as existed in olden times for finding styles of architecture and presenting them to the world. Architectural styles are indeed found, but only in the real sense when they are born out of the overall spirit of an epoch.

How can we today reach some understanding of the spirit of our epoch out of which alone the true architecture of the future can be found? I shall now try to approach the subject from quite a different angle and point of view.

An artistic experience destroyed by analysis and explanation

During the course of our work I have come across artists in many different fields who have a kind of fear, a kind of dread of spiritual knowledge, because spiritual science tries to open up a particular understanding of works of art and the impulses out of which they are created. It is quite true that efforts are made to interpret sagas, legends, and works of art, too, in the light of spiritual science, to explain the impulses underlying them. But so often it happens— and it is very understandable—that an artist recoils from such interpretations because, especially when he is really creative, he feels: 'When I try to formulate in concepts or ideas something that I feel to be a living work of art, or at least a fertile intuition, I lose all power of originality, I lose everything I want to express—the content as well as the form.'

I assure you that little has been said to me over the course of the years with which I have greater sympathy. For if one is at all sensitive to these things it is all too easy to understand the revulsion that an artist must feel when he finds one of his own works, or a work he loves, being analysed and 'explained'. That a work of art should be taken hold of by the intellect is a really dreadful thought for the artist who is present, somewhere, in all of us. A stench of death is almost tangible when we have an edition of Goethe's *Faust* before us peppered with the analytical foot-notes of some scholar. How ought we to regard these things? I will try to make the point clear to you, very briefly, by means of an example.

The Seven Wise Masters. An epic poem

I have before me the latest edition of the legend of *The Seven Wise Masters* published this year by Diederich.[13] It is an old legend of which many different versions exist. Fragments of it are to be found all over Europe. It is a remarkable story, beautifully and artistically composed. I am, of course, now speaking of the art of epic poetry, but the same kind of treatment might just as easily be inflicted on architecture. I cannot take you through all that is contained, sometimes in rather uncouth language, in this legend of the seven wise masters, but I will give you a brief outline of it.

A series of episodes, graphically narrated in connection with one main theme, commences with the words: 'Here begins the book which tells of Pontianus the Emperor, his wife the Empress and his son, the young Prince Diocletian; how the Emperor desired to hang his son on the gallows; and how he is saved by words spoken on successive days by Seven Wise Masters.'

An emperor has a wife and by her a son, Diocletian. She dies, and the Emperor takes a second wife. His son Diocletian is his lawful heir; by the second wife he has no son. The time comes for the education of Diocletian. It is proclaimed that this will be entrusted to the most eminent and wisest men in the land, and seven wise masters then come forward to undertake it. The Emperor's second wife longs to have a son of her own in order that her stepson may not succeed his father; but her wish is not fulfilled and she then proceeds to poison the mind of the Emperor against his son; finally she resolves to get rid of the son at all costs. For seven years Diocletian receives instruction from the seven wise masters, amassing a wide range of knowledge—sevenfold knowledge. But in a certain respect he has outgrown the wisdom that his teachers have been able to impart to him. He has, for instance, discovered a certain star in the heavens; and it is thereby intimated to him that when he returns to his father he must remain silent for seven consecutive days, must utter no single word and appear to be a simpleton. But knowing, too, that the Empress is intent upon his death, he asks the seven wise masters to save him.

The following now happens, seven times in succession. The son comes home, but the Empress tells the Emperor a story with the object of persuading him to have his son hanged. The Emperor gives his assent, for the story has convinced him. The son is led out to the gallows and on the way they come upon the first of the seven wise masters. When the Emperor holds him responsible for his son's stupidity, he—the first of the masters—asks leave to tell the Emperor a story, and receives permission. 'Very well,' says the wise master, 'but first you must allow your son to come home, for it is my wish that he shall listen to us before he is hanged.' The Emperor acquiesces and when they have returned to the palace the first of the seven wise masters tells his story. This story makes such an impression on the Emperor that he allows his son to go free. But the next day the Empress tells the Emperor another story, and again the son is condemned to death. As he is being led to the gallows, the second of the seven wise masters comes forward, begging leave to tell the Emperor a story before the hanging takes place. Again the upshot is that Diocletian is allowed to live. All this happens seven times over, until the eighth day has come and Diocletian is permitted to speak. This is the story of how the Emperor's son came to be saved.

The whole tale and its climax is graphically told. But now, think of it: we take the book and absorb ourselves in it; the graphic, if at times rather uncouth pictures cannot fail to delight us; we are carried away by a really masterly portrayal of souls. But such a story immediately makes people call out for an 'explanation'. Would this always have been the case? No indeed. It is only so in our own age, the fifth post-Atlantean epoch, when the intellect predominates. In the days when this story was actually written nobody would have been asked to 'explain' it. But the verdict nowadays is that explanation is necessary, and so one makes up one's mind to give it. Is it easy?

The story explained and analysed

The Emperor's first wife has given him a son who is destined to receive teaching from seven wise masters. His consciousness belongs to the times when people were still endowed with natural powers of clairvoyance. The soul has lost this clairvoyance but the human ego has remained—and can be instructed by the seven wise masters, who are presented to us in many different forms.

As I once said,[14] we have essentially the same theme in the seven daughters of Jethro, the priest of Midian, meeting Moses by the well belonging to their father; he eventually became the father-in-law of Moses. In the Middle Ages, too, there are the seven liberal arts.

The second wife of the Emperor represents the human soul as it is today, when it has lost consciousness of the divine and is therefore also unable to 'have a son'. Diocletian, the son, is instructed in secret by the seven wise masters and must finally be freed by means of the powers he has acquired from them.

We could continue thus, giving an absolutely correct interpretation which would certainly be useful to our contemporaries. But what of our artistic sense? I do not know whether what I now have to say will find an echo or not. When we read and absorb such a book and then try to be clever, explaining it quite correctly, in the way demanded by the modern age, we cannot help feeling that we have wronged it, fundamentally wronged it. There is no getting away from the fact that a skeleton of abstract concepts has been substituted for the work of art in all its living reality—whether the explanation is true or false, illuminating or the reverse.

The greatest work of art: Creation itself

Let us take this further. The greatest of all works of art is the world itself—macrocosm or microcosm. In olden times the secrets of the world were expressed in pictures, or symbols. We, in our day, bring the intellect, and spiritual science, too, to bear upon the ancient wisdom which has been the seed of the culture of the fifth post-Atlantean epoch. We do this in order to 'explain' the secrets of the universe. In comparison with the living reality this is just as abstract and barren as a commentary in comparison with a work of art. Although spiritual science is necessary, although the times demand it, nevertheless in a certain respect we must feel it to be a skeleton in comparison with the living realities of existence. It is indeed so. When only our intellect is kept busy by spiritual science and we draw up charts and coin all kinds of technical expressions, then spiritual science is nothing but a skeleton—especially when it is speaking of the living human being.

This begins to be a little more bearable when we are able to picture, for instance, the earlier conditions of existence on Saturn, Sun and Moon, the planetary epochs of Earth-evolution,[15] or the work of the several hierarchies.[16] But to say that the human being consists of physical body, etheric body, astral body and ego—or manas and kama-manas—is really dreadful; and it is even more dreadful to have blackboard charts of these things. Thinking of the human being in all his majesty, I can scarcely imagine anything more horrible than to be surrounded in a great hall by many living people and to have on a blackboard beside me at the same time a chart of the seven bodies of man.[17] But so, alas, it has to be—there is no getting away from it. It is, perhaps, not actually necessary to inflict upon our eyes these things which are anything but pleasing to look at—but we must have them before the eyes of our soul. That is part of the mission of our age. Whatever may be said against these things from the point of view of art or good taste, they are, after all, part and parcel of the times in which we live.

The destructive potential of spiritual science is to strip the world of its mysteries

How can we get beyond this dilemma? In a certain respect we do have to be arid and prosaic in spiritual science; we have to strip the world bare of its secrets and drag glorious works of art into the desert of abstract concepts, while admitting all the time that we are anthroposophists. How can we get out of this dilemma?

There is only one way. We must feel that spiritual science is for us a cross and a sacrifice, that in a sense it takes away from us practically all the living substance of world-secrets hitherto in the possession of mankind. I want to bring home to you the fact that compared with everything that truly lives, both in the course of human evolution and of divine evolution, spiritual science cannot but be like a field strewn with corpses.

The resurrecting power of artistic creating

But if we realize that pain and suffering are inseparable from spiritual science, in that it brings knowledge of what is greatest and most sublime in the world, so that we feel we have in ourselves one of the divine impulses of its mission—then spiritual science is a corpse which rises out of the grave and celebrates its resurrection. Nobody will rejoice to find the world being stripped of its mysteries; but on the other hand nobody will feel and know the creative power inherent in the mysteries of the world as truly as those who realize that the source of their own creative power flows from Christ, who, having carried the cross to the 'place of skulls', passed through death. This is the cross in the sphere of knowledge, which spiritual science carries in order to experience death and then, from within the grave, to see a new world of life arising. A person who quickens and transforms his very soul—in a way that the intellect would never approve—a person who suffers a kind of death in spiritual science, will feel in his own life a source of those impulses in art which can turn what I have outlined for you today into reality.

True spiritual perception is part and parcel of the aim before us—and we believe that the Building Association will help to make this aim understood in the world. I hardly think any other words are needed in order to bring home to you that the proposed building can be for anthroposophists one of those things which the heart feels to be a vital necessity in the stream of world events. For when it comes to the question of whether anthroposophy will find a wider response in the world today, so much more depends upon deed than upon any answer expressed in words or thoughts; very much depends, too, upon everyone contributing, as far as he or she is able, to the aim of our Building Association which is entering with such splendid understanding into the stream of human evolution.

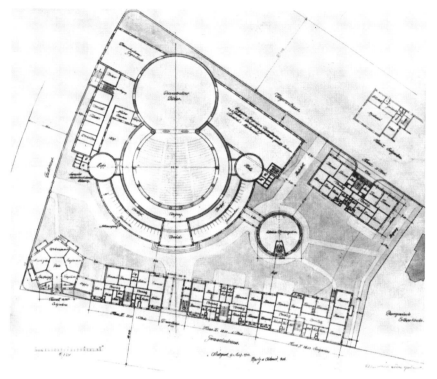

Site plan of Munich project, 1912

THE TASK OF MODERN ART AND ARCHITECTURE
As shown by a historical study of temple architecture and the accompanying development of the human soul

Lecture Two, Berlin, 5 February 1913

The new building as a necessity for modern times

During the last general meeting of the German Section of the Theosophical Society[1] here in Berlin, the Building Association[2] also held a meeting. On that occasion I indicated how our building was to become an integral part of artistic evolution as a whole and architecture in particular. I said that in line with other aspects of anthroposophy it was a necessary step within the spiritual and cultural evolution of mankind and not something invented by us in an arbitrary fashion. It is not an arbitrary ideal but a necessary continuation of what we can read in the script that reveals to us the progress of the human spirit during the course of earth evolution.[3]

This necessary step of placing our building within the stream of human evolution can be described from many points of view, of which I chose one on that occasion. Today another viewpoint will be considered in order to complement what I said here in December 1911.

Architecture is the art of creating an enveloping, enclosed space, with the help of a variety of materials and by means of various shapes and forms, either for ordinary activities and dwellings or for religious purposes. Therefore it is connected with the soul life of human beings. It originates from the soul, and it can be comprehended to the extent that the soul can be comprehended.

The three aspects of the human soul

During the course of our work in spiritual science the soul element has always been considered from three points of view, namely, those of the sentient soul, of the intellectual or mind soul, and of the consciousness soul. We also meet it, in a more tentative and as yet not so fully developed form, when we speak of the sentient body or the astral body. Finally, it appears again when we state that the soul has reached a stage of development in which it is seeking the transition to the spirit-self or manas. In my book *Theosophy*[4] there is a description of the threefold soul as the sentient soul, the intellectual or mind soul and the consciousness soul. In addition to that you will also find the sentient soul described as being next to the sentient body in a way that makes these two appear as two facets of one and the same thing, one of which belongs more to the soul and the other more to the spirit. Finally the consciousness soul and the spirit-self are paired together, again the one belonging more to the soul element and the other being more spiritual.

Two days ago our dear friend Arenson[5] gave a very satisfactory introduction to these concepts, showing how those who are truly immersed in anthroposophical work will want to go beyond the mere terminology of sentient soul, intellectual or mind soul and consciousness soul. They will want to ponder all these things in their heart and reach many, many ideas and feelings and views about how one aspect may be linked with other aspects, in order to achieve an overall understanding of all the variety of things these words can mean.

For spiritual vision they encompass whole worlds, so that new aspects arise which must also be taken into account, such as the sweep of evolution, even if we confine ourselves for the moment only to post-Atlantean times. We find that the sentient body underwent its development particularly strongly during the epoch of ancient Persian culture, the sentient soul during that of ancient Egyptian and Chaldean culture, the intellectual or mind soul in that of Greco-Roman culture, and the consciousness soul in our own time. We can now even discern the next epoch coming towards us, and with what we want to fashion through anthroposophy we can work on this new epoch, which is to show a connection between the consciousness soul and the spirit-self or manas.

The evolution of the soul reflected in architecture

I said just now that architecture was closely connected with the soul life of human beings. This naturally leads us to enquire whether architecture might not therefore also be connected with the evolution of soul life just described. If this were the case, would not the sequence of shapes and forms in architecture reveal characteristics that are in some way linked with the development of sentient body, sentient soul and so on? Then there would be no justification for speaking of architecture at all in relation to the first post-Atlantean epoch, when the ether body was being developed. For if architecture is closely connected with the soul life of human beings it cannot put in even a tentative appearance until that soul life begins to dawn. It could be expected to appear first of all in the age of the sentient body, since that is, in a way, the reverse side of soul life. Prior to that there would have been nothing that might correspond to today's definition of architecture.

It is difficult to delve into these questions from the point of view of ordinary history. Historical monuments and remains can hardly take us back beyond the epoch of ancient Egypt and Chaldea, so for any earlier times we have to fall back on clairvoyant research. Even the time of Zarathustra in ancient Persia lies beyond the reach of historical research, not to mention the epoch of the original Indian culture, which is the time connected with the development of the ether body. The Indian culture—even that of the Vedas—with which historical research is concerned, belongs to the third post-Atlantean epoch and parallels that of ancient Egypt and Chaldea. But what I am referring to here as the first post-Atlantean epoch is the original culture of ancient India, of which no external trace of any kind remains and of which the Vedas are a last vestige. It is described in my book *Occult Science*.

Early cave temples. From sentient body to sentient soul

In the first post-Atlantean epoch there can have been no architecture in today's sense. It was followed by a time when a definite step was taken which external history also mentions. The phase that preceded architecture was a time when chambers for religious purposes were built in caves or hollowed out of rocks. These are still to be found in India, but also in Nubia. It brings us to the very threshold of the time when the soul began to develop out of the bodily nature. These cave chambers bear out what spiritual science has to say about the evolution of the soul: only when soul development begins to evolve out of bodily development do we see architecture proper begin to evolve out of caves and subterranean chambers hewn into the living rock.

The living rock is like the human body into which the human soul has to work its way. The soul element has to work its way into the bodily element when sentient soul enters into sentient body. The transition from cave chambers to architectural structures enclosing human activities shows us the importance of the transition from the culture of the sentient body to that of the sentient soul.

A time will come when the riches of anthroposophy will be elaborated to cover all branches of human knowledge and all branches of human development. It will be found that all the things shown in a one-sided way by other world views have been knocked together out of inadequate concepts and ideas, while spiritual science, or anthroposophy, will reveal an overall view that can throw light into every corner. No matter that people do not believe this as yet. Time will show it to be true. Little by little proof will begin to appear in every sphere of life, including that of architecture.

The modern temple. From soul to spirit

By following the sequence of post-Atlantean epochs we can discover how they are linked to soul development, first the sentient soul, then the intellectual or mind soul, and finally, right up to our own time, the consciousness soul. We even see how in our time the spirit-self or manas begins to work its way up out of the consciousness soul and how we now face something like the opposite of that post-Atlantean epoch when the transition was made from the bodily to the soul element. Then the sentient soul worked its way out of the sentient body, whereas now the soul has to work its way once more into something spiritual. In architecture we have a similar contrast. Then, before architecture proper came into being, hollows were driven into the living rock. Now, when the task is to work our way into the spirit, we shall find the complement to this, its opposite.

The sentient soul. The Egyptian pyramid

Without working out the exact parallels in time—since this is something anyone can do—let us look at the sequence of developments brought about by the soul, beginning with the sentient soul.

By becoming endowed with the sentient soul, the human being enters into a mutual relationship with his environment. The realities present in this environment enter his inner being through the sentient soul. Anything that is outside is transformed into something that is inside via the experiences that take place in the sentient soul. What can we find in the development of architecture that arises naturally from cave building and is endowed with characteristics typical of the sentient soul? It would have to be something built in a manner that would allow what is outside to be represented inside. We only have to think of the pyramids and similar buildings. Even modern science agrees that in their measurements the pyramids have had astronomical and cosmic conditions incorporated into them. This is exactly what we are looking for. More and more discoveries are being made about the remarkable way the proportions of a pyramid depict cosmic situations, for example in the way the ratio of base to height represents certain cosmic measurements. More and more you come to sense that the priests of the pyramids expressed perceptions of cosmic relationships in terms of a building. It is as though the pyramid had been built so that the earth might experience within itself what can be perceived in the cosmos. The sentient soul brings to life inside itself what exists outside, depicting in its own way, within itself, what is there outside. In the same way the pyramid in its ratios of measurement, and in its shapes, repeats cosmic relationships, for example in the angles by which the sunlight enters in. Just as external reality is represented within the human being through the activity of the sentient soul, so does the pyramid appear like an enormous organ of sensation belonging to the whole of earthly civilization, through which it faces the whole cosmos.

The intellectual soul. The Greco-Roman temple

How would architecture appear in an age for which the intellectual or mind soul is characteristic? The intellectual or mind soul is the soul element in the human being that has most work to do within itself. On the inner foundation already created by the sentient soul it continues to expand this inner soul life, without however taking it far enough to consolidate it into the actual ego. It does not culminate in the central point of the ego. A person with this member of his soul in a particularly well-developed state manifests a great richness of soul life, full of the content and experience for which he has struggled. He would not feel particularly inclined to build up systems out of his inner experiences, but would prefer to revel in the wide sweep of all they bring to him. The intellectual or mind soul is self-sufficient; it is enclosed within itself, a life of soul that is inwardly whole.

What kind of architecture would be likely to arise from this? Unlike the pyramids, which reveal a kind of image or representation of cosmic relationships, it would have to be something enclosed within itself, its own totality. To suit the intellectual or mind soul it would show its breadth in all its parts but would not be much inclined to draw them all together. Without a doubt the architecture of Greece, and even of Rome, must be taken as a picture of the intellectual or mind soul.

We have often spoken of the Greek temple as the dwelling place for a god, the whole edifice forming an enclosed totality. We have noticed that the Greek temple does not need the presence of a congregation. As the dwelling place of a god it can exist as an entity in itself, just as the intellectual or mind soul is an inner entity, an inner life rounded off within itself, though not proceeding so far as to become an ego, yet being unconsciously a representation of the god in man. In the Greek temple some components bear down and others bear up, the columns rise up and carry the down-pressing weight of the cross beam; and all the many and varied forces form a totality without in any way seeking to create a unity or a culmination. In all this—and similarly, too, in Roman architecture—we recognize the breadth that characterizes the intellectual or mind soul.

Greek and Roman architecture is remarkable for its static quality, for the way all the individual forces—those bearing up and those pressing down—are in equilibrium. One thing that a Greek temple does not have is heaviness. If you have a feeling for nature you can gain the impression that the columns are growing up out

Erechtheum, Athens

of the ground, just as real plants growing up out of the ground give no hint of any pressure bearing down. That is why the columns in a Greek temple gradually evolved to resemble plant stems, though this only finally became obvious in the Corinthian column. The impression given by the columns is one of bearing up, not of weighing down. But once you reach the lintel, the architrave, you feel pressure weighing down. The whole building is in a state of perfect equilibrium. In the same way a person's soul life, if it is well-developed, gives a sensation of balance akin to the equilibrium between column and lintel in all the feelings, perceptions and concepts inwardly achieved. Greco-Roman architecture came into being at a time when the intellectual or mind soul was developing, so when the soul spoke in the language of architecture it gave expression as a matter of course to the equilibrium of its inner experience. That architecture came to reflect the soul life of that time was not intentionally planned; it simply arose out of the way the human soul poured itself into the architecture.

The consciousness soul. The Gothic cathedral

Then the consciousness soul began its gradual evolution. In essence its nature is to summarize everything in one overall feeling that says: 'I am this one single human being, this one personality,

Sainte Chapelle, Paris

an individual in my own right.' When we live in the intellectual or mind soul we sense the god living within us; we feel how the god lives in every vibration of our soul. Because we are sure of his presence we have no need to gather him together to a point at which we might say: 'I and the god within are one.' In the consciousness soul, however, this is necessary, for here we are not at rest within ourselves as we are in the case of the intellectual or mind soul. In the consciousness soul we strive to go out of ourselves in order to bring our ego purposefully into reality and existence.

If you are sensitive to language you will have noticed how the very words just spoken about the consciousness soul are inclined of themselves to depict a Gothic pillar or a Gothic arch. We now have before us a building that does not express inner balance but endeavours to use its forms to escape from mere in-built equilibrium. There is a tremendous difference between a lintel whose weight is carried in static equilibrium by its columns and an arch brought into being by mutual support from either side. Here everything tends upwards into a point, just as the force of the human soul gathers itself together in the consciousness soul.

Sensing the progress of human evolution, particularly in Italian and French architecture, we discover the transition from the development of the intellectual or mind soul to that of the consciousness soul. It is no longer a matter of static equilibrium in bearing up and weighing down in total balance, as was desirable in Greek architecture, where inner uniformity was the aim. The struggle now is to achieve a dynamic escape from our enclosing skin and enter, like the consciousness soul, into contact with external reality. In tall windows Gothic arches open up to the light of the sky. For a Greek temple the presence or absence of light is of no particular consequence, but a Gothic cathedral is unthinkable without light refracted by the stained-glass windows.

We can sense how the consciousness soul places itself into the world as a whole, how it struggles to enter into general existence, and how Gothic architecture is therefore characteristic of the age in which the consciousness soul is developed.

The next step in human evolution. The new architecture

This brings us to our present time in which a way of looking at the world is striving to come into being, not in an arbitrary manner but as the necessary next step in human evolution. This way of looking at the world must bring us to the realization that it is time for the human being to work his way from the soul element into that of the spirit, until in the spirit-self he comes to rest within himself. Gothic architecture seems to presage this process in its walls interspersed with windows that are open to what wants to enter in, and now must enter in. The Gothic cathedral is like a forerunner of what is to come. Whereas in the Greek temple the walls enveloped the whole, in the cathedral they are broken up and function as filling and decoration between the windows. This is a forerunner of what must now come into being as a home for the new way of looking at the world. I have already described it to some extent and have even tried to put some aspects into practice, for example in our building in Stuttgart.[6]

What is now needed is essentially a complement to the preliminary stage of architecture, when caves were hewn in rock, so that the rock itself formed the boundary to what was hollowed out in it. Our new building will be as though open on all sides, not literally open in a material sense, but open to the spirit. We shall achieve this by shaping the walls in a way that will let us forget that there is an everyday world outside our building. I have already

An oval 'temple space', Stuttgart 1911, by Rudolf Steiner

attempted this in the Stuttgart building; although they are made of solid material, its walls are open to the spirit. In our new building we shall accomplish the shapes and forms, the decorations and paintings in a way that breaks through the walls so that through the colours and the shapes, though they are made of solid material, we shall be able to see into the universe with eyes of spirit and soul. The pyramids incorporated the measurements of the cosmos. Similarly we shall use all that we can experience through anthroposophy as a means to give to the walls such shapes and colours, contours, forms and figures as will make them disappear. What encloses us will everywhere give us the illusion of expanding out into the cosmos, into the heavenly spaces, just as the consciousness soul passes from the merely human realm into that of the spirit when it enters into the spirit-self.

The proposed new building in Munich

In the new architecture individual columns will advance to a new significance. Since inner equilibrium was the main emphasis in the Greek temple it was obvious that each column and each capital should be a repetition of the one before. As each column had exactly the same weight to carry as its neighbour there was no point in changing its shape.

In our new building it will be a matter of going out into a universe that is various and different on all sides. We are to forget that we are enclosed within an interior space, so the columns will have to fulfil an entirely new task. Each will be like a letter of the alphabet reaching out beyond itself to form a word with other letters. The columns will not be arbitrarily varied but will combine like individual letters to form a significant script pointing outwards to the cosmos, pointing outwards from within. This is how we shall build: from the inside outwards. As one capital follows on from another they will combine to express a wholeness. This will lead out beyond the interior space.

Similarly, in other parts, for example the cupolas, we shall apply the paintings in a way that does not give us a feeling of being enclosed but of being able to look and go beyond, right

Interior sketch, Munich project, 1912

into the depths of infinity. To do this we shall have to learn to paint like Johannes Thomasius, whose work makes Strader feel: 'I would like to break through this canvas to find what I should seek.'[7]

A new architecture that overcomes physical substance

We shall come to see that no word in the Mystery Dramas is superfluous, that each forms an integral part of the whole, and that all the things we want to achieve on the basis of present-day culture are linked together. Today I wanted to give you a feeling of how our new architecture will have to represent an overcoming of physical substance in the whole way the walls, the architectural motifs, the columns, and all the decorations are treated. Walls will have to be overcome so that they open up outward-looking perspectives; mural paintings will also have this task. I wanted to give you a feeling of the fact that all this will have to come about and be attempted through our new architecture; and that this is necessary,

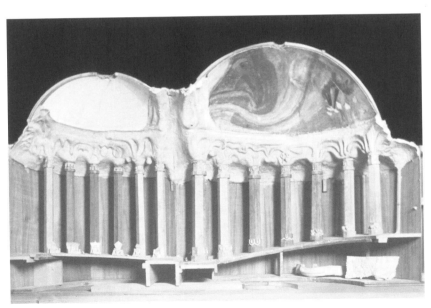

Interior model for Dornach by Rudolf Steiner, 19 October 1914

given the process of human evolution that will have to take its course.

The very fact that a building of this kind must of necessity arise out of human evolution makes the difficulties that are being placed in its path look very pathetic. The authorities in Munich have raised objections and so have members of the artistic fraternity they have consulted. They say the building will stifle its neighbours. Perhaps with foreboding in the pit of their stomach they sense how the building will indeed point the way to the far future. For the moment they feel inwardly stifled by it.[8]

Seen from the perspective of human evolution, the objections of the artistic fraternity, who consider themselves to be representatives of the pinnacle of artistic achievement in our age, are indeed grotesque and ridiculous. But let us hope, while doing what we can on our own account, that our guardian spirit will take pity on us so that, knowing how necessary our building is, we shall soon indeed be in a position to create a suitable dwelling place for anthroposophy or spiritual science.

Rudolf Steiner with his exterior model for Dornach, 16 June 1914

OUTLINE PROPOSALS FOR THE ARCHITECTURE OF A MODEL ANTHROPOSOPHICAL COMMUNITY AT DORNACH

Lecture Three, Berlin, 23 January 1914

Freedom of initiative, a prerequisite

Now that the construction of the Goetheanum[1] is under way at Dornach, a number of our members are hoping to set up home nearby, and some have already enquired about sites, with the intention of building private houses in which to live all the year round, or at least for part of the year. What I now want to say in this connection should not, of course, be interpreted as a wish on my part to interfere in any way with what these people intend to undertake in the vicinity of the Goetheanum. It should be clearly understood, in keeping with the way we interpret our anthroposophical movement, that the freedom of each individual member must be respected to the utmost. Thus it is not my intention even to hint at any sort of compulsion. I may, however, be permitted to express what would be desirable.

In the first place we shall have, at Dornach, the Goetheanum itself. We have tried to find a way of building originating in a truly new approach that can express, in architectural forms, what we are aiming at. So at long last we may create something which will not only represent a dignified but also an appropriate home for our work.

The first new buildings indicate a way forward

Dr Grosheintz[2] has shown you illustrations which demonstrate the efforts that have already been made to achieve this goal. If the funds prove adequate, other buildings will, as you have just seen, arise in the immediate vicinity of the Goetheanum. The attempt will be made to carry these out so that they represent an artistic unity with the plans for the Goetheanum itself.

Boiler House 1913/14, design by Rudolf Steiner

A number of factors have to be considered before such a 'whole' can arise. So far we have only been able to put this idea into practice in the case of one little building which you can see here in the model.[3] Initially this building is to be used for the engraving of

The Glass House from the west, design 1914 by Rudolf Steiner

the coloured glass windows. It will be large enough also to house Herr Rychter[4] and perhaps one other person.

Form follows function

The Boiler House,[5] which has already taken on a fairly definite form, is a second undertaking in this plan. The problem has been to design this large chimney to be both architecturally in keeping with the main Goetheanum building and constructed in reinforced concrete. It would obviously be a monstrosity if it were to resemble those normally put up.

From the small model and the illustrations shown to you by Dr Grosheintz you will see that the attempt has been made to solve the architectural character of this building. When it is completed, and particularly when the heating plant is in operation—the smoke has been thought of as part of the architecture—it will be possible to feel that this chimney has a beauty of its own. This will be despite its prosaic function, by virtue of the fact that its task is expressed in its shape—even though this shape has not arisen

The Boiler House, 1914

according to utilitarian architecture as conceived hitherto, but as the result of an aesthetic design process. The two small domes link up with the rest of the structure and the chimney. The rising forms on the latter have been thought to resemble leaves by some, or ears by others. But there is no need to define them so long as they are appropriate. The Goetheanum and directly adjacent buildings will be heated from here and the forms will show that a building

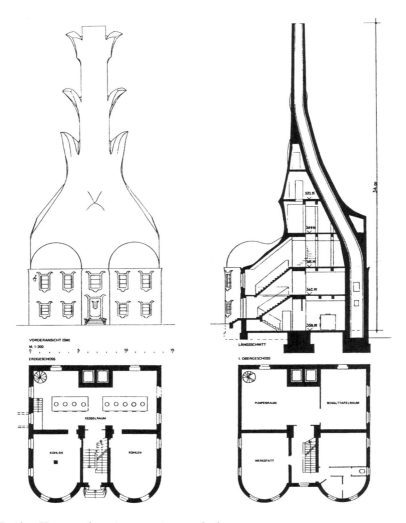

Boiler House, elevation, section and plan

serving the modern requirements of central heating can at the same time be aesthetically satisfying.

In a task of this sort it is necessary first of all to have exact particulars both of the purpose of the proposed building and of what is to take place in it. If you know how many rooms are required and what purpose they are to serve, how many types of vertical communication there are to be, as well as what orientation and outlook the client requires, and if you also know the exact site and how the building is to relate to the Goetheanum, to the north or to the south of it, then I would claim it is possible to find an appropriate architectural solution for every such scheme.

Visual unity of the community

One essential consideration therefore, if we are not to sacrifice our principles, is that it really will be necessary for those friends who want to join the community and build in the neighbourhood of the Goetheanum to make common cause, at least in the wider sense, with what must be attempted in the case of buildings immediately surrounding it. Through the outer appearance, through the whole style of the buildings, it should become apparent to the world at large that all these houses belong together and form a connected whole. Even if other houses are situated among them, it would still be desirable that those put up by members of the anthro-posophical community should be so built that one can tell by looking at them that they form part of a greater whole. The out-side world may even say 'What peculiar people'. Let them! What is important is that they can notice this—be it approvingly or disapprovingly. Even if this complex of buildings belonging to the Goetheanum is interspersed with other houses, we want to give cause for people to notice that it comprises an ideal whole.

A home for spiritual science must reveal its essence

A further consideration is that we do want to create something that has a real bearing on the cultural development of the present day. From the forms of the Goetheanum itself you can tell that we want our spiritual scientific approach to enter into archi-tectural style as well as into artistic practice in every field of

*Goetheanum terrace
looking west to House
Grosheintz (Duldeck)*

activity. If asked, for example, about the best way of practising the art of dance we have to seek our own contribution and will come to eurythmy.[5] The same goes for other forms of art. We need to find our own artistic contribution and thus produce something in the world for those who want to understand. Perhaps this is only possible for a spiritual stream that is as fruitful as spiritual science.

I have often mentioned an address given by Heinrich Ferstel,[6] architect of the *Votivkirche* in Vienna and rector of the technical university there. He maintained that architectural styles are not invented. One can argue strongly against this tenet, and one can also prove it to be correct. Both arguments have their logic. Perhaps styles of architecture are indeed not invented, but it does not follow from the rightness of this contention that one can simply take the Gothic style as Ferstel did and put up the *Votivkirche* in the form of a somewhat enlarged example of the confectioner's art. Nor does it follow that architectural styles nowadays may only be created out of eclectic combinations and modifications of past styles.

First Goetheanum from the south-west

It is precisely the approach to this problem, based on spiritual science, which should show that it is possible to infuse architectural design with true art forms born of an inner, spiritual life. We should prove to the world that this is also possible in the case of private houses. This is an angle that ought to win some understanding for our work, and in showing that we are able to approach such tasks from this point of view we will create meaningful values for the culture of our time.

Cooperation and social endeavour

Hence, although influencing anyone's freedom would be inappropriate, it would indeed be fine if members of the community were, out of their own free will and filled with a recognition of our fundamental principles, to club together to create a homogeneous whole. We have to accept the fact that an existing house,[7] which cannot at the moment be removed, is situated quite near to the Goetheanum and will not exactly enhance the beauty of the site. But although we cannot aim to make everything entirely beautiful, we ought to see to it that what we ourselves do is beautiful in accordance with our understanding.

I cannot help admitting that I have been really depressed recently, after some building plans came to my notice proposing house designs for members of the community. They undoubtedly

House Grosheintz 1914 from the west, design by Rudolf Steiner

House Grosheintz from the east

arose from the best intentions, but they nevertheless exhibited all the monstrosities, all the revolting features of a ghastly style of architecture. Given the requisite good will, there must surely be other ways of doing things. Obviously there will be hindrances and difficulties, but what new venture striving to make its way in the world does not encounter hindrances and difficulties?

Although I do not intend to interfere tomorrow when the members of the community form their association,[8] I nevertheless feel that the prospects will be dim if this leads to anything that goes against what has just been expressed. If we all take the greatest of care, it will be possible to achieve the aim described. But if members of the community lack the patience to wait until a good solution can be found for a given dwelling, then nothing favourable will be able to come about.

However easy it may be to understand that some are in a hurry to get their building project under way, it would still be desirable if those who are in earnest about our aims could exercise patience, so that things can be carried out in accordance with intentions that cannot be described as having foundations in our own will, but which must be called forth through spiritual science.[9] It is quite possible that something may arise that will appear comical in the eyes of the world. Let them laugh! It will stop eventually. If one were never to undertake anything of this kind there would never be any progress in human evolution.

The harmony of outer forms as a reflection of the harmony within the resident community

There is no need to worry that anyone would have to suffer the slightest discomfort in his or her house if the principles I have outlined are adhered to. One thing, however, will be essential, and that is that members of the community do not all go their several ways, but that what gets done is done in harmony; that one can talk things over and rely on one another. The architectural features that will cause the whole community to appear as an ideal unity will be an external imprint of a harmony of an inner kind. I now want to say something that is partly a wish and partly a hypothesis: all the built forms of the community should be an expression of the inner harmony of its inhabitants.

House de Jaager from the west, design 1921 by Rudolf Steiner

House de Jaager from the north-west

So far as the aims of the Anthroposophical Society are concerned, it will be impossible for the faintest trace of discontent or
mutual incompatibility or even an unfriendly word to pass from
one member of the community to another—let alone any wry
glances. It will be wonderful when the very harmony of the

external forms suffuses everything like a personification of peace and contentment. Forms stimulate thoughts, so even if some should find reason to pull a face or adopt a grim expression, they will regain their contented smile as soon as their eyes alight on these sociable, peaceful forms.

Truly organic solutions must be differentiated

All these factors taken together certainly give us reason to strive for a homogeneous result. Do not believe for one moment, however, that the unity will oblige one house to be exactly like another. On the contrary, the houses must be varied and they will have to be very individual in character. Just as there would be nothing organic in putting an arm or hand where the head ought to be in a human body, so a house that would be right for one site would be wrong for another. All this will have to be very carefully thought through for our purposes.

Control of occupation within the community

Apart from setting all this in train, there will still be various other points to take into account. Consider that while we have

Houses for eurythmists, from north-west, design 1920 by Edith Maryon and Rudolf Steiner

been gathered here this week, a society of theosophists met in the next room on Monday, and another society on one of the other days.[10] This is all very well. But now imagine that the son or daughter or grandchild of one of our members were to join a different society and then later inherited one of the houses in our community. No longer would we just be sharing premises for lectures in a neighbourly way, for now the different views and attitudes of that society would be present in our very midst.

We must begin now to consider the difficulties that might arise in the course of time, and how such difficulties are to be met. This could only be achieved if an association of members of the community were able to find ways and means to retain the properties of members of the Anthroposophical Society for other members. It will become clear to you during the discussion of practical principles tomorrow that this can only be achieved through the adoption of certain definite measures. Naturally heirs should not suffer, but it is nevertheless possible, without prejudicing heirs, to make sure that one's property within the community cannot be inherited by any heir who is not a member of the Anthroposophical Society.

It would be most desirable to maintain this community into an indefinite future as one for members of the Anthroposophical Society. But it would not be at all in keeping with our spiritual movement only to have in mind how pleasant it is to be able to live there oneself, how nice it is not to have too far to go to performances and lectures in the Goetheanum, and how enjoyable it is to be among fellow anthroposophists. That our spiritual movement still requires a certain degree of sacrifice becomes doubly clear the moment the necessity arises to translate its principles and impulses into practical reality. It is more or less self-evident that we cannot have our houses built by architects at random; and it should be equally clear that we will try to preserve the anthroposophical character of the community.

These are aspects of the matter that I wanted to lay before you, not in order to exert pressure, but as something which, on closer inspection, you will admit cannot be avoided if any significant results in the service of the Goetheanum building and thus of our anthroposophical concern are to be achieved at all.

An opportunity to create a model community

We had to abandon Munich, as you know, because we met in the first instance with absolutely no understanding for our artistic aims. In Dornach, where we are to be allowed to settle, we can put ourselves in a position to create a model for what our spiritual stream has to offer the future. We would be misunderstanding our movement if we did not want to do this, if we allowed petty considerations to prevent us from keeping to the views we have just discussed. Everyone who wants to build there ought to see the necessity of joining an association of the residents of our new Dornach community. Perhaps the best thing of all would be if the artistic side of the matter, in particular, were to be made subject to a kind of commission. There is no need to force this issue, but how splendid it would be if all the members of our new community were to agree to put everything destined to arise there in the hands of such a steering group.

Members of our community would then really be able to carry out our intention of filling a whole group with a common will and purpose, to be guided in the direction mapped out by our anthroposophical approach. In this way something really exemplary might arise in Dornach, and the result would show how well or how badly our cause had been understood. Every ugly house put

House Schuurman from the west, design 1924 by Rudolf Steiner

up by one architect or another would be further proof of how little is understood as yet of our anthroposophical movement, while every house expressing our anthroposophical way of thinking in its forms would give rise to pleasure at this proof that at least some individuals do have an understanding of what we want to achieve!

A contribution to the world at large

It is my great wish to see the fulfilment of my intentions for this general meeting, and I still hope that we may make progress tomorrow on the questions of how each one of us might work amongst our fellow citizens in an anthroposophical way, and of how we could best show our attitude and place our experience at the service of society at large. Perhaps we can still have a really stimulating discussion about this. If we mean to gain ground in the world for our movement, it is not enough merely to show, on its own, the wisdom to be found in anthroposophy. In what we create in Dornach we must take pains to embody, for the world to see, what is given to us in the form of spiritual knowledge, just as older styles of architecture embodied bygone cultures.

If we are successful in creating something truly homogeneous in Dornach, and also in providing full legal security for it as the preserve of the anthroposophical movement, then we shall have offered proof of the fact that we have understood the aims of our

Transformer Station from the east, design 1921 by Rudolf Steiner

movement. Let us hope that architectural and other artistic forms of many kinds will begin to prove to us that anthroposophy as such is being properly understood.

Most emphatically we do not want to be a sect or some group or other asserting its dogmas. We want to be something that takes cultural tasks seriously. So far as the Goetheanum and the buildings surrounding it are concerned, we can only do this if we act in accordance with what has been said.

Roofscapes of House de Jaager and Second Goetheanum from south

PART II

WAYS TO A NEW STYLE OF ARCHITECTURE
In which all the visual arts are united

TRUE ARTISTIC CREATION

The common origin of the architectural forms in the Goetheanum and of the Greek acanthus motif

Lecture One, Dornach, 7 June 1914

True art strives to be in harmony with its stage in human evolution

A thought that may often arise in connection with the Goetheanum building is that of our responsibility to the many sacrifices which dear friends have made for its sake.[1] We can only respond through a strong sense of responsibility towards achieving the actual fulfilment of the hopes being invested in this building.

Anyone who has seen even a single detail—not to speak of the whole structure, for no overall conception of that is possible yet—will realize that the architecture represents a complete change from other architectural styles which were considered fitting in their own stage of evolution. An undertaking like this can of course only be justified if the goal is attained in some measure. In comparison with what might be, we shall only be able to achieve a small, perhaps insignificant beginning. Yet perhaps this small beginning will reveal the lines along which a spiritual transformation of artistic and architectural style must come about in the more distant future.

We must realize, however, that once the building has been completed it will meet with all manner of criticism, particularly from so-called experts who will state that it is unconvincing, perhaps even amateurish. This will not disconcert us, for it lies in the nature of things that 'expert' opinion is least of all right when anything genuinely new is placed before the world. We shall, however, not become dispirited in the face of derogatory criticism levelled at our idea of artistic creation if we realize—as a kind of consolation to back up our sense of responsibility—that it is precisely in our age that the origin of the arts and the origin of their particular forms and motifs is being misinterpreted by professionals. Gradually we shall understand that all we are striving to attain in this building stands close to those primordial forces of artistic endeavour which are revealed when the eye of the spirit is directed to the origin of the arts. This is in contrast to the conceptions of art that claim to be authoritative at the present time. There is now little understanding of what was, in earlier ages, a true conception of art. It need not therefore astonish us if a building like ours, which strives to be in harmony with the primordial will and in accord with the origin of the arts, is not well or kindly received by those who adhere to the tendencies of the present age.

To make this clearer let us consider a well-known artistic motif, the acanthus leaf. I would like to show you how our own aims are in harmony with the same artistic endeavour of mankind that led so long ago to the acanthus motif, though our endeavours, being separated by thousands of years from the first appearance of this motif, will naturally lead to something quite different from the acanthus leaf that came to be a part of the Corinthian capital.

The modern materialistic conception of art

Speaking personally, if I may, I would like to mention that I spent my student days in Vienna at a time when the civic buildings, which have given that city its present stamp, were being completed—the Parliament, the Town Hall, the *Votivkirche* and the *Burgtheater*. The famous architects[2] of these buildings were all still alive: Hansen, who revived Greek architecture, Schmidt, who elaborated Gothic styles with great originality, and Ferstel, who built the *Votivkirche*. The *Burgtheater* was designed by Gottfried Semper who in the 1870s and 1880s was the leading influence in artistic appreciation and development of form in architecture and sculpture. One of my teachers at the university, Joseph Bayer,[3] an excellent and talented writer on aesthetics, was an admirer and disciple of Semper. I was thus surrounded by the whole conception of the world of architectural, sculptural and decorative form as inaugurated by that great man.

In spite of all the talent at work at that time, there was something in the whole atmosphere emanating from current conceptions of historical development, and from the way art was being created, that could almost drive one to despair. Semper was

First Goetheanum from the south

undoubtedly very gifted, but in those days the usual conception of the human being and the universe was an outcome of the materialistic interpretation of Darwin,[4] and this doctrine of evolution was also apparent in current ideas of art. Again and again this materialistic element crept into conceptions about art. You had to learn all about the techniques of weaving and wickerwork. First the weaving of fabrics and the plaiting of fences had to be studied, and from these techniques architectural forms were derived. People were force-fed with the principle that decoration and ornamentation had evolved from the techniques of the craftsman.

This could be further elaborated, but I only wish to indicate the general trend that was asserting itself at the time, the trend of tracing everything artistic back to the techniques of craftsmanship. People's standpoint was one of utilitarianism, and the artistic element was considered to be a direct outcome of the function for which objects were intended. Wherever artistic themes, in particular ornamentation, were spoken about, the discussion was concerned with the techniques of craftsmanship.

This paralleled the great flood of materialistic conceptions that swept over the nineteenth century. It was a materialist's conception of art. The extent to which materialism asserted itself in all spheres of life during the second half of the nineteenth century was enough to drive anyone to despair. I still remember how many sleepless nights the question of the Corinthian capital gave me.

The main feature of the Corinthian capital, its principle decoration—although 'decoration' was virtually a forbidden word at the time of which I am speaking—is the acanthus leaf. What could be more obvious than to infer that the acanthus leaf on the Corinthian capital and elsewhere was simply the result of a naturalistic imitation of the leaf of the common acanthus plant? A sensitivity for art, however, should make it very difficult to accept that somewhere along the line a beginning was made by taking the leaf of a weed, an acanthus leaf, making a carving of it and sticking it on to a Corinthian capital.

Let me draw a rough sketch of the leaf of *Acanthus spinosus*, the ordinary spiny acanthus:

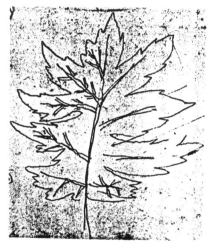

Acanthus leaf by Rudolf Steiner from his notebook, June 1914

This is supposed to have been carved in stone and then added to the Corinthian capital.

Vitruvius on the origins of the Corinthian capital

Here we have to remember Vitruvius,[5] the scholarly cataloguer of the artistic traditions of antiquity. He quotes a well-known anecdote which led to the adoption of the 'basket hypothesis' in connection with the Corinthian capital. The capitals of Corinthian columns did indeed gradually come to be seen as baskets held in place all round by acanthus leaves.

What is the story? Vitruvius relates that Callimachos, the Corinthian sculptor, once saw a little basket standing on the ground somewhere with acanthus plants growing around its base. So Callimachos, we are told, looked at a little basket surrounded by acanthus leaves and said: Here is the Corinthian capital! Who could imagine anything more materialistic? I will tell you in a moment the real significance of this anecdote narrated by Vitruvius.

The point I am making is that in the course of our modern age all understanding of the inner principle of artistic creation has gradually been lost. If this understanding cannot be rediscovered, people will simply never grasp what we intend by the forms we are creating, such as the forms of our capitals or indeed of our whole building. Those who hold fast to the basket hypothesis will never be able to understand.

The need to rediscover the inner principle of artistic creation

The basis of all artistic creation is to be found in a state of being or consciousness which existed before the beginnings of recorded history. This was a particular consciousness that was active in human beings at the dawn of historical times, and was a remnant of an old human clairvoyance. This state of being also belongs to the fourth post-Atlantean epoch, the age of ancient Greece and Rome.[6] Although ancient Egyptian culture belongs to the third post-Atlantean epoch, all that was expressed in Egyptian art belongs to the fourth epoch. By the time of the fourth post-Atlantean epoch this consciousness gave rise to inner feeling in a way that made human beings able to perceive how human movement, bearing and gestures developed the human form and figure out of the etheric into the physical.

To understand what I mean, try to imagine that in those times, when there was a true comprehension of artistic will, the actual sight of a flower or tendril was far less important than the feeling: I have to carry something heavy, I bend my back and generate with my own form the forces that make me, a human being, shape myself in a way that will enable me to bear this weight.

Human beings felt within themselves what they had to bring to expression in their own gestures. One movement was used to grip hold of something, while another was an expression of carrying; stretching your hands out in front gives you a feeling that you are carrying something. Out of such gestures arose the lines and shapes leading over into art. Within your own human nature you can sense how the human being can go beyond what eyes see and other senses perceive by becoming a part of the universe as a whole. You take up a position in the universe as a whole when you notice that you cannot just saunter along when carrying something heavy. Out of a feeling for lines of force, which one has to develop inwardly, arises artistic creation. These lines of force are nowhere to be found in external reality.

The sun and the earth motif: an ancient ritual

When engaged in spiritual research one often comes upon a wonderful akashic picture[7] depicting the joining together of a number of human beings into a whole in an ordered and harmonious way. Imagine a kind of stage surrounded by an amphitheatre filled with spectators. In the centre people are walking round in a procession. This is not supposed to create a naturalistic impression in the spectators but a sense of something lofty or indeed supersensible. Seen from above it would look like this:

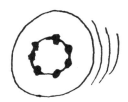

And the side view would show a group of people walking in a circular procession one behind the other, surrounded by the spectators.

These people portray something of great significance, something that does not exist in the physical world but can only be expressed in analogies. They portray something that brings human beings into connection with the macrocosm. In those times it was a question of representing the relationship of the earthly forces to those of the sun. How can this relationship come to be felt? It is like feeling the carrying of a load. Earthly things rest squarely on the ground, but when they endeavour to wrest themselves free—if you imagine the forces necessary for this—a pointed shape emerges. The human being's state of being bound to the earth is therefore expressed by a shape that has a wide base and runs upwards to a point. Sensing these forces, people felt that they were standing on the earth.

In a similar way they also became aware of their connection with the sun. The sun works downwards towards the earth, and they expressed this by portraying the lines of force raying inwards, just as the sun, in its apparent journey round the earth, sends its rays down towards a mid-point.[8]

These two alternating representations give you the earth motif and the sun motif carried in antiquity by the people who formed the circling procession. Round them sat the spectators, and in the centre the actors passed around in procession, alternately one with the earth motif and one with the sun motif, whose raying-in can also be described as a striving-outwards of sun forces.[9]

Initially this force, this cosmic tension of earth and sun, was felt, and only subsequently did people begin to consider how they might portray it. The best medium for the purposes of artistic expression proved to be a plant or tree whose forms run upwards to a point from a wider base, alternated with palms. Plants having a form like a wide bud were alternated with palms. The palms represented the sun-forces, and bud-forms running upwards to a point, the earth forces.

The palm chosen as an expression of the sun forces

People learnt to feel their position within the cosmos and created, so to speak, certain form relationships. Subsequently, on reflection, they selected certain plants as a means of expression, instead of having to create artistic objects for the purpose. The choice of suitable plants was the artistically creative act which was in turn the result of a living experience of cosmic connections. Thus the creative urge in human beings is no mere wish to imitate things in the world around them. The artistic representation of natural things only became a part of art at a later stage. When people no longer realized that palms were used to express the sun forces, they began to think that the ancients had simply imitated palms in their designs. This was never the case; the people of antiquity used the leaves of palms because they typified the sun forces. All true artistic creation has arisen from a superabundance of forces in the nature of the human being—forces that cannot find expression in external life and which strive to do so through our consciousness of our connection with the universe as a whole.

In both science and art, considerations and perceptions have been misled and confused by a certain idea which will be very difficult to erase. It is the idea that complexity must arise from simplicity. This is just not true. For example, the construction of the human eye is much simpler than that in many of the lower animals. The course of evolution is often from the complex to the simple, so that the most intricate interlacing finally resolves into a straight line. In many instances, simplification is the later stage, and we will not acquire a true conception of evolution until we realize this.

Primeval experience condensed to an ornamental motif

What people sensed in those ancient times, and what was presented to the spectators seated round about as a depiction of living, cosmic forces, was later simplified into ornamental lines summarizing what had once been a living experience. The complexity of human evolution honed down into the simple lines of an ornamental border might be drawn like this:

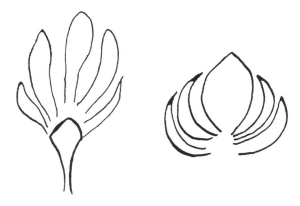

In the alternating patterns you have a simplified reproduction of those people circling in procession with earth motif, sun motif, earth motif, sun motif and so on. What human beings felt and experienced in those ancient times is here summarized in an ornamental border. This decorative motif was already a feature of Mesopotamian art, and it is also found in Greek art as the so-called 'palm motif', either in this form or a similar one, resembling the lotus petal.

This alternation of earth and sun motif presented itself to the artistic feeling of people as a really decorative ornamental theme in the truest sense. Later on it was forgotten that in this decorative ornament they were looking at an unconscious reproduction of a very ancient dance gesture, a festive, ceremonial dance. Nonetheless, this fact has thus been preserved in the 'palm motif'.

The Doric capital

It is interesting to consider the following. Among the painted

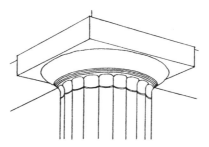

Doric capital

decorations of some Doric capitals you often find an intriguing motif which I will sketch thus. Beneath the weight borne by the capital is the torus, and below that we find the 'palm motif' as a painted theme showing the earth and sun motif in a somewhat modified form going round the whole top of the column. Above is the Doric torus, and below it, painted right round the top of the column, the ornamental motif as a decoration. In this way some Doric columns actually show the 'palm motif' painted beneath the capital like the procession of alternating earth and sun motifs.

Earth, Sun, Earth

The Ionic capital

In Greece, where the fourth post-Atlantean epoch found its fullest expression, all that came over from Asia, together with what I have now described as decorations on Doric columns, became united with the dynamic architectural principle of weight-bearing as such. This union came about because it was in Greece that the ego was most perfectly realized within the human body, and

Ionic capital

therefore this design motif found expression in Greek culture. The ego, when it is within the body, must grow strong if it has to bear a load. You feel this in the volute:

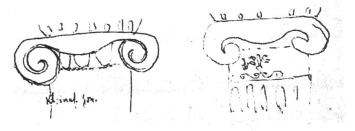

Ionic capitals by Rudolf Steiner, from his notebook, June 1914

It is this feeling of strengthening which is experienced in the volute. It was particularly in the fourth post-Atlantean epoch that the human ego was being strengthened; this is found expressed in the volute. Thus we arrive at the basic form of the Ionic capital. It is as though, unseen within the capital, Atlas is bearing the world on his shoulders,[10] and the volute becomes the weight-bearer.

You need only imagine the middle portion, which is merely indicated in the Ionic capital, developing downwards to become the complete volute, and you have the Corinthian capital. The middle portion is simply extended downwards, so that the character of weight-bearing becomes complete. Then think of this weight-bearing in the form of a sculpted figure, and you have the human force bent over in itself—the ego bent over, bearing the weight here:

Corinthian capitals by Rudolf Steiner, from his notebook, June 1914

The Corinthian capital

We can speak of an artistic principle when we have a large-scale motif that can be repeated or reproduced in miniature, or vice versa. Imagine the Corinthian capital with the main volute bearing the abacus, and repeat this artistic motif lower down where it only serves as an ornament. The result all the way round the base of the capital is a sculptural reproduction of the whole thing as a decoration. Now imagine the painting on the Doric capital, which grew out of the decorative representation of a very ancient motif, being united with the decoration on the Corinthian capital. Imagine sensing the wish to recreate in relief

Corinthian capital

what used to be only painted, and you will find the painted motif reappearing in relief form. I can illustrate this for you by the diagram of the palm motif. The urge arose to bring the 'palm motif' into the later decorative motif. Here it was not a motif representing the bearing of a load; what was mere painting in the Doric capital, and therefore flat, was sculpted in the Corinthian capital and the palm leaves were made to turn downwards. On the left I have drawn a 'palm motif', and below it the beginning which arises when the 'palm motif' is worked out in relief [see drawing opposite]. If I were to continue, the painted Doric 'palm motif' would metamorphose into the Corinthian sculpted 'palm motif'. The 'palm motif' when it is sculpted becomes the so-called acanthus leaf.

The acanthus leaf arises when the 'palm motif' is worked out in relief.[11] It is the result of an urge not to paint the 'palm motif' but to work it out in high relief. The weight bearer became increasingly elaborate until it began to give people the feeling that it resembled the acanthus leaf, and so this is what they came to call it, although it has nothing to do with any such thing. Thus the whole nonsense about the motif being a naturalistic representation of an acanthus leaf is exposed. What is now called the acanthus leaf did not arise out of naturalistic representation at all, but out of a metamorphosis of the ancient sun motif, the 'palm motif', being sculpted instead of painted. So you see that these artistic

Corinthian capital, Tholos

forms have proceeded from an inner perception of the gestures within the human ether body, the flowing lines of force connected with every movement.

Art cannot arise by imitation of the external world

Art in its essence can no more arise from an imitation of nature than music can be created by imitating nature. Indeed even when art is imitative, the thing that is imitated is fundamentally secondary, an accessory, and thus naturalism in itself is absolutely contrary to true artistic feeling. If the shapes and forms in our art here are thought by others to be grotesque, we will be able to draw comfort from the knowledge that the artistic conceptions that find our art grotesque are those that see in the acanthus motif nothing but a naturalistic imitation. In reality it is drawn from the spirit and only in its later development came to bear a remote resemblance to the acanthus leaf. Artistic comprehension in future ages will simply be unable to understand this attitude of mind which in our time influences not only the art experts, who are supposed to understand their subject, but which also dominates artistic creation as such. The materialistic attitude of mind in Darwinism also confronts us in artistic creation where there is a growing tendency to turn art into a mere imitation of nature. Insight into the origin of the acanthus motif has given me much joy, for it proves circumstantially that the primordial forms of artistic creation have also sprung from the human soul and not from imitation of external phenomena.

Understanding art comes from doing art

I was only really able to penetrate to the essence of art after I had myself created the forms of our building here. Feeling the forms, moulding them out of the very well-springs of human development, leads to a sense of how artistic creation has arisen in human evolution. It is a remarkable karmic situation that during the time when I was deeply engaged in pursuing a certain artistic intuition, which had arisen during the General Meeting in Berlin in 1912, I began to investigate what I had created in these forms in order to arrive at a deeper understanding of them—this was after the forms of our building had already been designed.[12] You can only think afterwards about artistic forms. If you understand them first and then carry them out they will be of no use at all; if you create on the basis of concepts and ideas nothing of value will ensue. The very thing that I perceived so clearly in connection with the acanthus leaf, and what I proved to be erroneous about it, is an indication of the inner connections between the spiritual science which will be active within our building and those things which it will express artistically.

Alois Riegl on the origins of the Corinthian capital

Just occasionally there are signs that these things are also understood elsewhere. Alois Riegl[13] appears to have reached the same conclusion, that the so-called acanthus leaf developed from the 'palm motif', though he failed to realize that 'palm motif', too, is merely a word behind which the reality of the sun-earth motif is hidden. He referred to the Vitruvian anecdote about Callimachos but omitted to say that the basket Callimachos saw was on the grave of a young girl. By mentioning this location Vitruvius was implying that Callimachos was a clairvoyant who saw above the girl's grave the sun forces struggling with the earth forces, and above this the girl herself floating in her pure etheric body. Here we have a hint of how the sun-earth motif came to be depicted on a capital. By seeing with clairvoyance what is actually present above the grave of a young girl you can come to understand how the 'palm motif' can be transformed into the acanthus leaf. It grows up all around the ether body of the young virgin which rises up in accordance with the sun laws. The same is depicted in the 'Clytie' portrait showing the bust of a noble Roman woman which appears to be growing out of a flower.[14] This is a late Roman statue showing what a clairvoyant may see above the graves of certain people.

We shall not understand what really underlies the anecdote

'Clytie', portrait of a Roman woman c. AD 40

quoted by Vitruvius until we have outgrown the unfortunate habit of asking what everything means and of always looking for symbolic interpretations showing how this, that or the other depicts the physical body, the ether body or the astral body. Once this habit has been eradicated from our movement we shall come to understand what really underlies artistic form. It is either a direct perception of how one moves spiritually or it is a perception of the corresponding etheric movement.

The form surface of the Goetheanum

All this goes to show that in order to understand the forms in the interior of our building—the forms that are to adorn it—we first have to reach an understanding of the artistic principle from which they have arisen. In trying to understand the principle of the interior space formed by our two half domes, or, more correctly, three-quarter domes, we could do worse than imagine how a jelly-mould works.

The jelly-mould and the jelly

The jelly takes shape inside the mould and when the mould is upturned and removed, the jelly reveals all the forms that are present in negative inside the mould:

The same principle may be applied in the case of the interior design of our building, only here there is no jelly inside but the living word of spiritual science moving and weaving in the form possible for it. All that is enclosed within the spatial shapes, all that is spoken here and done within them, must adapt to them as the jelly adapts to the negative forms of the jelly-mould. We should feel the walls as the living negative of the words that are spoken and the deeds that are done in the building. That is the principle of the interior design here. Think of the living words of spiritual science as they come up against these walls, hollowing them out in accordance with their profundity of meaning. They hollow out shapes that fit their meaning. This is why these interior forms are shaped as they are, worked out of the flat surface.

I at least felt from the outset that it was right to work with gouge and mallet in such a way that the chisel was struck with the left hand from the start in the direction in which the surface is to lie when it is finished. So we strike in this direction from the start. On other occasions we hold the gouge at right angles to the surface.

I would have preferred it greatly if a surface like this one [*pointing to one of the architraves*] could have been avoided. It will not be right until this round part here has been removed. It would have been better to work with a gouge from the start,[15] for then there would have been no bulge but only a surface. What we must do is feel from the models how the interior shaping is the garment, the sculpted garment for the spiritual science that is given to us in this building. Just as the interior shaping has the quality of being hollowed out from the inner surface, so will the outer shaping be something that is laid upon the outside. Inside there must be a sense of having been hollowed out. Working on the model I was able to sense this. It was a matter of finding an inner sense for a shape enclosing a space.

This is why even Adolf Hildebrand's book leaves one dissatisfied on this score.[16] He certainly has ideas about the effects forms can have, but what he lacks is an ability to feel his way right into the forms themselves. In his opinion they are something you look at with your eyes. Here [*pointing to a form*] you should experience the form within yourself so that, holding the gouge in a particular way, you grow to love the surface you are creating, the surface that is coming into being here under your mallet and gouge. I must confess that I cannot help caressing a surface like this once it has been created. We must grow to love it, so that we live in it with inner feeling instead of thinking of it as something that is merely there for our eyes to look at.

The seven woods of the interior

The other day I was told, after a lecture, that some bright spark

Interior of First Goetheanum under construction showing the 7 capitals in

had complained about the way we attach such importance to details in the physical world, as shown, for example, by the way each of the columns is made from a different wood.[17] This shows how little our work has been understood. Even this very intelligent person cannot understand that the columns have to be made from different woods. He has not paused to consider what answer he would give if he were asked why a violin has different strings. Why not simply use four A-strings? The use of different woods is a reality in precisely the same sense. We could no more use only one kind of wood than we could have only A-strings on a violin. Our concern is with real inner necessities.

One can never do more than mention a few details in these matters. The whole conception of our building, and what must be expressed in it, is based upon immense wisdom, but a wisdom that is at the same time very intimate. The forms in it are obviously nowhere to be found in the physical world. Any apparent resemblance in our building to shapes found in animals or in the human body arises from the fact that higher spirits, who work in nature, create in accordance with the same forces with which we are creating; nature is expressing the very things we are also expressing here in our building. It is not a question of imitating nature

7 different timbers with architraves above

but of expressing what exists as pure etheric form. It is like asking how I would imagine myself if I were to leave the external world of sense-perceptions out of account and seek instead surroundings that would express in forms my own inner being.

Intimate relationship between the whole and each part

I am well aware that the sculpted forms of the capitals and the rest of the interior will meet with some criticism. Nevertheless, every single one of these shapes has its own *raison d'être*. Someone working on this column down here [*pointing*] with mallet and gouge will carve more deeply than up here. It would be nonsense to demand symmetry. There must be living progression, not symmetry.[18] Everything about the columns and architraves in the interior is a necessary consequence of having the two cylinders of the building—one smaller, one larger—surmounted by the two intersecting domes. I cannot express this any more precisely than by saying that if the radius of the small dome were any larger or smaller in proportion to the large one, then each of these forms would have to be quite different, just as the little finger of a dwarf is different from that of a giant.

It was not only the differences in dimension, but the differences in the forms themselves that called forth an overwhelming sense of responsibility for making everything just as it is now, down to the smallest detail. Each separate part of a living organism has to exist within, and in accordance with the whole. It would be nonsense to want to change a nose and put another organ in its place. Similarly a big toe as well as a small toe would have to be different if the nose were different. Just as no one in his senses would wish to remodel the nose, so it is impossible that any form here should be other than it is. If one form were changed the whole building would have to be different, for the whole is conceived as a living, organic form.

What was once instinctive needs to be brought to consciousness

What was, in the early days of art, a kind of instinctive perception of human gestures transformed into artistic form must now enter with consciousness into the feeling life of human beings. This is the

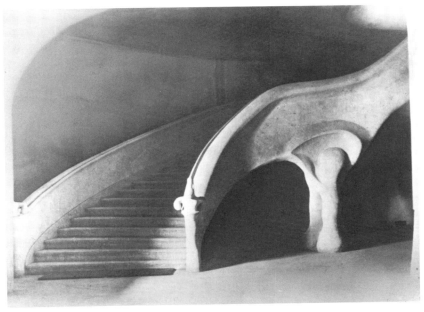

The First Goetheanum, west staircase leading to main hall

step forward to be taken in our time. In this way we shall have, in our interior designs, etheric forms that are truly alive, and we shall feel how all that is to live in these spaces must make its impression precisely in this way. It simply cannot be otherwise.

Recently I received two letters from a man who used to belong to our anthroposophical movement, though he left it about ten years ago.[19] He wanted to be allowed to design the windows of our building, insisting that he was very well qualified to do so. But when you see the windows you will understand that they could only be made by someone who has followed our work right up to the present. Just as the impression of my hand in clay will not look like an ox's head, so must the true impression of our spiritual science show in our interior design, and so must our spiritual science let in the sunlight through the windows in a way that harmonizes with its own nature. As we have said, the whole building is constructed according to the principle of the jelly mould, only in place of the jelly it is filled with spiritual science and all the sacred things that inspire us. This has always been the case in art, and above all it was so in the days when human beings perceived in their dim, mystical life of feeling the alternation of the principles of earth and sun in the living dance, and then portrayed the dance in the 'palm motif'. So it must be when it is a question of penetrating the sense-perceptible shell of natural and human existence and expressing in forms things that lie behind the realm of sense perception—if, that is to say, we are fortunate enough to be able to carry this building through. How inner progress is related to onward-flowing evolution will be perceptible in the building, in its proportions, its forms, its designs and paintings.

I wanted to present you with these thoughts so as to help you avoid being misled by modern conceptions of art, which have put all true understanding on one side. A good example of this is the belief that the Corinthian capital is supposed to depict a little basket with acanthus leaves around it. The truth is that something springing from the very depths of human evolution has been expressed in the Corinthian capital. In the same way we shall feel that what surrounds us in our building is the expression of something living in the depths of human nature, behind the experiences and events of the physical plane.

Today I only wanted to speak about this aspect of our building and, in connection with this, about a certain chapter in the history of art.

Other opportunities might present themselves in the coming weeks to speak to you of other things in connection with some of the motifs in the building. I shall seize every available opportunity, and any situation that presents itself, to approach the complex but spiritually natural and necessary foundation on which our building rests.

Genuine art only resembles itself

Nowadays it is not at all easy to speak about artistic questions, for naturalism, the principle of imitation, really dominates the whole realm of art. So far as the artist himself is concerned, naturalism has arisen out of a very simple principle, though for other people it seems to have arisen from something less simple. While he is training, the artist must, of course, imitate the works of his teacher in order to learn something. But people today have an instinctive feeling that they do not want the situation of authority implicit in the pupil-teacher relationship, so in the place of the teacher they put nature, which they imitate instead. It is easy for the artist not to go beyond imitating what he sees in front of him; and for the layman naturalism is a matter of course.

Where on earth can ordinary people find any clues by which to arrive at ideas about forms like those they see in our building? They will tap their forehead and shrug their shoulders, considering themselves lucky if they find anything at all to take hold of, such as some detail that remotely resembles a nose. Although this may be negative, they are delighted to have discovered anything at all. Since all the arts nowadays lack anything that might point to what lies behind nature, lay people are likely to be thankful for anything they can find that resembles something they recognize. This confusion that leads to art being seen as something resembling nature is understandable. But genuine art does not resemble anything at all; it is something in itself, sufficient unto itself.

Artists seeking to imitate what they see

As a result of the materialism of the second half of the nineteenth century, painters, not to mention sculptors, set themselves no more than the task of getting effects, such as that of mist in the distance. All kinds of attempts were made to reproduce nature by pure imitation. It was really enough to drive one to despair. Paintings of real genius were produced, but to what purpose? It is all far better in nature itself. The artists were wasting their time in their efforts to imitate, for nature has it all in a much higher form. The answer is to be found in the Prologue to *The Portal of Initiation*.[20]

Genuine sculpture is conceived purely in terms of itself

Recently, at an exhibition in the Luxembourg Palace in Paris, we saw a statue that was quite difficult to make out. By degrees it dawned on us that it might be meant to represent a human figure. It was so distorted—I will not imitate the posture for it would be too much of a strain to make a shoulder indistinguishable from a knee. It is a hideous object, but I assure you that if one were to meet it in nature it would be much easier to understand than as a so-called 'work of art'. People today do not realize the absurdity of making a sculpture out of something that has been thought out, for in that case there is, in fact, no real necessity to make it into a sculpture. A sculpture must contain within itself that which is to be sculpturally expressed and it must be conceived of purely in terms of sculpture.

No real sculptor would count as sculpture some of the things that Rodin has produced.[21] Rodin is a sculptor of themes that are not sculptural. His work is that of a genius in an external sense, but anyone with a genuine feel for art must ask whether it amounts to anything, for a true sculptural conception is entirely lacking.

All this is connected with an overall materialistic, naturalistic conception of art. I have told you what happened when I was twenty-four or twenty-five when I was studying Semper and his concepts. Even then these drove me to despair, and nothing has changed to this day.

True art is born from the depth of our being

Therefore I ask you—and more particularly those of you who are working so devotedly and unselfishly on our building, with all the sacrifices this entails—always to try to proceed from an inner feeling for what this building ought to contain, and to feel in life itself the forms which must arise in order that we may free ourselves from the trammels of much so-called modern 'art'. We must realize in a new sense that true art is born from the depths of our being. This is so little understood today that people have taken the metamorphosis of the earth and sun motifs to be an imitation of the acanthus leaf. If people would only stop believing the anecdote quoted by Vitruvius that Callimachos saw a basket surrounded by acanthus leaves and then used it as a motif on capitals, and would instead listen to what he says about Callimachos having seen a vision above the grave of a Corinthian girl, they would realize that he had clairvoyant sight; and they would have an understanding of the evolution of art. They would realize that the development of clairvoyance leads human beings to the realm that lies behind the world of the senses. They would also realize that art is the divine

The First Goetheanum from south, under construction, 1 April 1914

child of clairvoyant vision—although it only lives as unconscious feeling in the soul—and that the forms that are beheld by the clairvoyant eye, in the higher worlds, cast their shadow pictures down to the physical plane.

When, through our building, people actually want to understand what it is that lives in the spirit and has the power to impress itself on our building as it encompasses us, finding expression in the outer framework around us, then they will also understand the goal we have set ourselves. They will see in the various artistic expressions the imprint of what has to be accomplished and proclaimed in living words in our building. This building of ours speaks in living words!

Now that I have endeavoured, though scantily, to indicate something about the interior, we shall soon be able to speak about the paintings and also about the exterior.

ART AS THE CREATION OF ORGANS THROUGH WHICH THE GODS SPEAK TO US
The First Goetheanum as an example of such an organ with its windows showing the path to the gods

Lecture Two, Dornach, 17 June 1914[1]

The task and the sacrifice

Even more than on the last occasion when I spoke to you about our Goetheanum building, I am today reminded of the attitude we must adopt with regard to it, dedicated as it is to the cause of spiritual science. The sacrifices of those who have befriended the cause of anthroposophy call for a sense of great responsibility, and today is a splendid occasion for reminding ourselves of it, for the first of our auxiliary buildings is to be given over to its own special tasks. The immediate use to which these rooms will be put is the engraving of the glass windows for our building.

We cannot but be moved by the thought that our human faculties are not as yet really mature enough to accomplish the full task before us. I think it is healthy and good that all our work should be permeated by this feeling that we have not as yet grown equal to our task. This alone can enable us to accomplish the highest that lies within our power. We shall be able to create the first beginnings of an artistic garment for spiritual science—to the extent that the present time and our present means allow—if we always acknowledge the feeling that we are, in truth, little qualified for the full task. The site on which our building stands is pervaded by an atmosphere that seems to say: Do the very utmost of which your powers and faculties are capable, for you cannot do nearly enough in comparison with what ought to be achieved; and even when you have done your very utmost, it will not by any means suffice.

The glass engraving studio as part of a larger whole

When we step on to the site of our building we ought to be

The Glass House from south

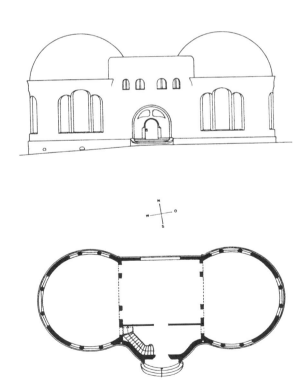

The Glass House, south elevation and ground floor plan

encouraged by an indefinable feeling of being confronted by an immense task. More particularly should this be the case today as we hand over this auxiliary building to our friend Rychter[2] and his colleagues—to their souls, in the first instance—so that they may carry out artistic work here that may grow to be an organic part of the whole organism of our building.

Entering the room through this door we feel blessed and privileged to work on creating the glass windows here. When we think of the task that is to be fulfilled by these very windows, an atmosphere of soul and spirit will hover around us, whispering of the deep spirituality which we pray may flow like purifying waves of healing through this room.

The main building to transcend everything personal

It may very well be that when the main building is finished we are frequently assailed by a depressing sense of the need to grow beyond everything personal, if there is to be any meaning in having forms like these as a framework for our spiritual science. A satisfying aspect of our building—and our architects, engineers and all the members working on it may share this satisfaction—is that despite, all the cares and toil that it involves, it can be a wonderful education in transcending everything personal. It demands a great deal more than the expression of any personal element for, as we set about our work and permeate the single forms with thought and feeling, we become conscious of new tasks of which we previously had no inkling. We sense some mysterious force governing us, calling to our highest forces of soul, heart and mind to create something that transcends personality. This building can teach us how to set ourselves tasks through what arises around us every day. It brings home to us a feeling that rings out in sacred tones in our soul, telling us how much greater than little human beings are the potentialities of the universe, how much greater must become the best that we can produce from within ourselves if it is to cope with the tasks facing us in the objective world. All that can ever be contained within the limits of the personal self must be transcended.

Our building itself, and also this auxiliary building which we have been able to open today, can be a means of education for us,

Plate 1a. Red and blue. A copy, from memory, made by the painter Hilde Boos-Hamburger of Rudolf Steiner's blackboard drawing made during his lecture of 26 July 1914.

Plate 1b. Form gesture for the Second Goetheanum. Blackboard drawing by Rudolf Steiner made during his morning lecture of 1 January 1924.

Plate 2. First Goetheanum. View into Auditorium from lobby in west showing base of Saturn pillar. A pastel sketch made in the building by Wilfred Norton.

Plate 3. The First Goetheanum. Inside Auditorium looking west with both Saturn pillars and organ loft between, by Wilfred Norton.

Plate 4. First Goetheanum. Interior base of Moon pillar, north side, by Wilfred Norton.

Plate 5. First Goetheanum. Interior looking between two thrones on to the stage and beyond into the auditorium, by Wilfred Norton.

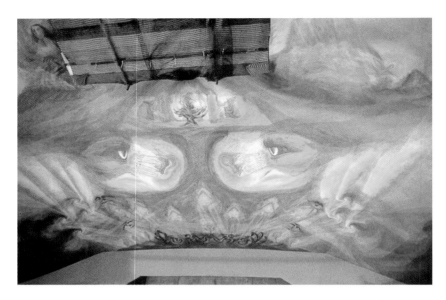

Plate 6a. Second Goetheanum. Auditorium ceiling painting looking west showing the creation by the Elohim of eye and ear and Paradise. Executed 1997 under the direction of Christian Hitsch, based on Rudolf Steiner's designs.

Plate 6b. Second Goetheanum. Auditorium, top of architrave and ceiling paintings, Lemuria and Ancient Indian epochs. Executed 1997 under the direction of Christian Hitsch, based on Rudolf Steiner's design.

Plate 7. Second Goetheanum. Auditorium north wall, Moon and Sun pillars with architrave, flanked by green and blue engraved windows. Windows by Assja Turgenieff, executed 1928; architraves and pillars executed 1997 under the direction of Christian Hitsch, all based on designs by Rudolf Steiner.

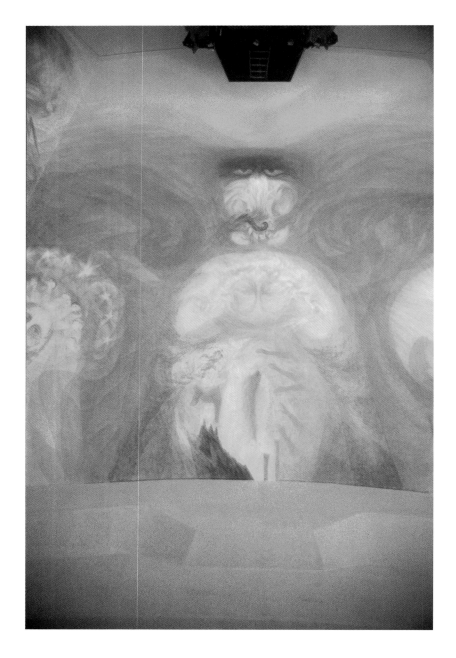

Plate 8. Second Goetheanum. Auditorium ceiling immediately above proscenium arch in the east. 'EAO' executed 1997 under the direction of Christian Hitsch, based on designs by Rudolf Steiner.

and the more it is our teacher the better will be our relationship to it. Even now, when we step inside the unfinished building, or inside these rooms which are a kind of continuation of the main building, we cannot help wondering what our feelings will be as we enter. Shall we not often long to bring all the human beings in the world into these rooms? Do we really deserve such a framework for what we cherish so highly, a framework on which we ourselves have worked, if we seek to exclude other people? Shall it not rather be our dearest wish to bring all human beings into this building, and especially those—if it should find imitators and followers—whose task it will be to build other such buildings for all mankind?

True art and architecture as lawgivers

We will now pass to something else that is closely related to this. A great many buildings have been erected in our time by brilliant architects, and some of them, although they show no signs of a new style and are not permeated with any new spirituality, are certainly creations of architectural genius. But they all have one thing in common. We may admire them from outside and think them beautiful inside, but they do not make us feel, as will our building, that we are encompassed in the way we are encompassed by our own sense organs. The reason for this is that these buildings are mute—they do not speak. I would like to elaborate on this tonight.

Let us observe buildings that express all the characteristics of our time. We experience people passing in and out without in any way being able to unite with the architecture, the forms or the artistic conception. We experience that what ought to be expressed through the artistic forms has to be communicated to people by other means instead. In our present time we see an increasing need to use external laws, external regulations and institutions, all of which fall under the heading of 'decrees', to create order, security, peace and harmony. This statement implies no syllable or thought of criticism, since this is how things have to be in our time. But something must be added to this, something that signifies the onward evolution of humanity in a different sense. It is unlikely that all this will be achieved by our building, for we are only making a modest beginning. But we shall have fulfilled the task set us by the gods if, in the future, human culture is able to adopt what is expressed in our building and develop it further. If the ideas underlying such works of architecture find followers in human culture, then people who enter such buildings and allow themselves to take in what speaks through artistic expression, and who learn to understand its language with their heart, and not only with their intellect, will never wrong their fellow human beings. The artistic forms will teach them how to love. They will learn to live with their fellows in peace and harmony. Peace and harmony will pour into hearts through these forms. Such buildings will be 'lawgivers'. And their forms will achieve what external measures can never achieve.

Art and architecture as the larynx of the gods

However much study may be devoted to the elimination of crime and wrong-doing in the world, true redemption, the turning of evil into good, will in future depend upon whether true art and architecture are able to generate a definite cultural atmosphere, an atmosphere that can so fill the hearts and souls of human beings—if they allow this atmosphere to influence them—that liars will cease to lie and disturbers of the peace will cease to disturb the peace of their fellow citizens. Buildings will begin to speak. They will speak a language of which people today have as yet no inkling.

Nowadays people gather at congresses to negotiate world peace. They imagine that speaking and listening can actually create peace and harmony. But peace and harmony will never be established through congresses. Peace and harmony, and conditions worthy of humanity, can only be established when it is the gods who speak to us. When will the gods speak to us?

We had better first ask: When do human beings speak to us? They speak to us when they have a larynx. Human beings would not be able to speak to us without a larynx. What the gods of nature have given us in our larynx we can pass on to the whole of the world when we find appropriate artistic forms, and through these forms the gods will speak to us. We only need to understand how we can enter into this great process. If we achieve this understanding it will increase our longing to bring the whole of humanity in through these doors. Out of this longing, which cannot as yet be fulfilled, will grow the desire to work so intensely for our spiritual movement that this aim may gradually be attained.

Art is the creation of organs through which the gods will be able to speak to mankind. I have already spoken of many things in this connection, for instance of the Greek temple and how all its forms were created to express the fact that it is a dwelling place for the god.[3] Today I want to add something to this.

The Greek and Roman temple

If we try to understand the basic form of ancient Greek architecture we shall realize that the very being and essence of the fourth post-Atlantean epoch[4] flowed into the Greeks' mode of perception and experience and in consequence into their architecture. What is the basis of ancient Greek perception and experience? What is its foundation? Certainly it cannot be described in a few words, but let me speak of one particular aspect.

Here we have the wall enclosing the Greek temple [*drawing on the blackboard begins*], with the horizontal structure resting upon it. Whatever is placed above this horizontal is so constructed that it rests in its own forces as when, in construction, we place a beam upon two supports like this.

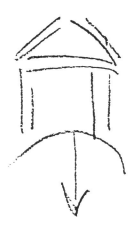

What is the presupposition of this system? It is that the earth with its gravity is felt and experienced to be down here [*the arrow*

is drawn]. Translating this feeling into words, we could say that in the fourth post-Atlantean epoch people sensed that the god had made a gift to them of their place on earth and had poured divine forces into their artistic activity, so that gravity can be overcome by using the forces the gods have given to human beings along with the earth. The god, who has donated the earth to humanity, is given a dwelling place that has been created by means of utilizing the force of gravity.

This dwelling place of the god is inconceivable without the Greek landscape surrounding it, just as the later Roman temples are inconceivable without the surrounding countryside. They belong together. I have already pointed out that a Greek temple is complete in itself even when there are no people inside it, for its whole conception is that of the dwelling place of the god, whose statue may stand within. People are all around in the countryside. No one enters the temple, yet it stands there, complete in itself—a dwelling place of the god. In every detail we see how people expressed in the decorative forms of these dwelling places of the gods all that their feelings of veneration made them believe they ought to do for the gods. You will recall that in my last lecture I attempted to show you that the motif on the capitals has its origin in the motif of a dance that was performed as homage to the gods of nature. Thus, in the Greek capital, first in painting and then in relief, people applied to the dwelling place of the god what they themselves imagined and felt to be for the glory and veneration of the gods.

The Christian church and the Greek temple

Let us now pass on to the forms of the earliest Christian architecture. One thought in particular must arise when we pass from the Greek temple to the Christian church.

The Greek temple stands within its surrounding territory; it belongs to the territory. The people are not inside the temple; they live around it. The temple belongs to the countryside and is thought of as the sacred place of the countryside. It hallows everything, even the most ordinary daily occupations of the people who live round about. Service rendered to the earth becomes a service rendered to the gods because the god stands or sits in his dwelling place as the ruler. The god participates in the work on the land and in the pursuits of the people living around the temple. People feel united with the god as they work on the surrounding land. Worship of the god is not yet separate from service to the earth. The temple grows out of the human element, sometimes indeed out of the all-too-human element, participating in all the good and not-so-good things that go on all around it. 'Earth—be firm!' This is the prevailing mood during the fourth post-Atlantean epoch, when human beings are still one with the earth which the gods have given into their charge, when the human ego is still slumbering in a kind of dream consciousness, when human beings still feel connected with the group soul of the whole of humanity. Then gradually they grow away from this group soul, becoming more and more individual: they separate the worship they perform in their spiritual life from the land, from daily life and activity.

In the early days of Christianity people's feelings were no longer the same as in the Greek age. We see the Greek sowing his fields and working at his trade, pervaded by the unshakable feeling: There stands the temple and the god is within while I am nearby; I may follow my trade and work on the land, and all the while the god is dwelling there within the temple.

The early Christian and Romanesque church

But then the human being became more of an individual; a stronger sense of ego arose within him. Something that had been prepared through the course of long ages by the ancient Hebrew civilization now emerged particularly in Christianity. Out of the human soul there arose the need to separate off from the affairs of everyday life the worship that was offered to the god. The sacred building was separated from its surrounding territory, and the Christian church came into being. The territory became independent, and within it the building became independent, a territory in itself. Whereas the Greek temple was an altar for the whole surrounding countryside, the walls of the Christian church now excluded these very surroundings. A space was set apart for those who worship. The forms of Christian churches, including those of Romanesque architecture, gradually came to express this individual, spiritual need of the human being, and we can only understand these buildings when we view them from this point of view. Because of the way the individual Greek lived in his body on the earth he said: 'I can remain here with my flocks, plying my trade and doing my work on the land, for the temple stands over there like an altar for the whole countryside; and within it dwells the god.' Then through Christianity a different feeling arose in the human being and he said: 'I must leave my work and trade, for the god has to be sought in there, inside the church.' Earthly worship and heavenly worship became separated. Architecture gradually adapted to the human being's need for individuality and thus Christian churches increasingly took on a form that would have been quite unsuitable for Greco-Roman times. It is a form which reveals that the congregation belongs inside it; and gradually separated from the congregation was the part set aside for the priests and the teachers. An enclosed world arose within a world that had itself already been enclosed within walls. Here the spirit spoke to those who sought the spirit. The feeling of the Greeks and Romans for the whole world was the same as that felt by the Christians for the space within their church. What the Greek temple as a whole had been, now became the chancel with the altar. An image of the world was sought in the forms of church architecture, whereas in earlier times people took the world as it was and only added what was not visible to the physical senses, namely, the dwelling place of the god.

The Gothic church

Gothic architecture is, essentially, only a branch of what had been prepared earlier. Its main feature is that the bearing of weight is transferred from the walls to the pillars.

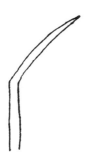

What is the origin of this whole mode of construction, where the weight rests on the pillars, which are so formed that they are able to bear it? The system of construction of the Greek temple is based on quite a different conception. It is as though the human being had got to know the force of gravity inside the earth; and then, finding himself placed on the surface of the earth, he makes use of gravity, and by doing so overcomes it. That is the Greek temple, which is the dwelling place for the god. In the weight-bearing pillars of Gothic architecture, on the other hand, we are no longer concerned with the effects of gravity as such but with the work of the human being. Gothic architecture requires individual craftsmanship. The wish to create an enclosed world for the congregation gives rise in Gothic architecture to the need to create something wherein the activity of the congregation plays a part. What the people of the congregation have learnt is embodied in the forms they create. The art of the craftsmen flows into the Gothic forms, and in studying these forms we see the work of human beings who have all worked together contributing their share in the town community.

In older Romanesque churches the building is intended to enclose the congregation as well as the god. In Gothic churches we have a building built by the congregation to enclose the god and to which the craftsmen have added their contribution. They do not only go to church but as a congregation they also share in building it. In Gothic architecture the labour of human beings unites with the divine. Their souls no longer receive the divine as a matter of course; they gather not only to listen to the word of the spirit proceeding from the altar but also to work together and bring to their god what they have learnt. Gothic churches are really crystallized craftsmanship.

The Renaissance

We can quickly pass over what came next, since it merely amounted to a revival of Greco-Roman architecture. For our present purposes there is no need to speak about the Renaissance. So let us turn to what the fifth post-Atlantean epoch demands of us.

The design motif of the Goetheanum

Please observe carefully the element of support and weight in the Greek temple. Follow it to the point where it becomes crystallized craftsmanship in Gothic architecture. If we penetrate it with our artistic feeling we realize that the Greek temple is something at rest within itself, at rest within the earthly forces. Fundamentally all the forces of these buildings rest within the earthly. Especially in the Greek temple, wherever you look you will observe the force of gravity in union with the earth. Throughout the Greek temple you can study aspects of gravitational force at work. Its very forms reveal its union with the earth.

Imagine now the fundamental form in our building here, a form that will confront people from outside as they approach. Here is a rough sketch of it:

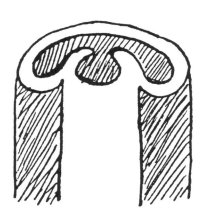

What is essentially characteristic about this design motif? If you compare it with the Greek temple you will discover the difference. The Greek motif is complete in itself. If it is a wall, it is just a vertical wall. Our motif here, on the other hand, is not merely a wall, for it only has meaning if it comes 'alive' and is not just a static wall but allows things to 'grow' out of it. Here the wall is not merely a wall, it is alive, just like a living organism that allows elevations and depressions to grow harmoniously out of itself. The wall has come alive—that is the difference.

The First Goetheanum, west front

However many columns there are in a Greek temple, the whole is none the less governed by gravity. In our building, however, nothing is mere wall. The essential thing is that forms grow out of the wall. When the time comes for us to walk about inside our building we shall find many sculpted forms, a continuous relief joining the capitals, and other forms on plinths and architraves. What is their significance? It is that they grow out of the wall, and the wall is their soil without which they could not exist.

In the interior of our building there will be a great deal of such relief carving in wood. Forms which, although they are not to be found elsewhere in the physical world, represent an onward flowing evolution. Beginning with a few forceful bars between the Saturn columns at the back, there will be a kind of symphonic progression of harmonies culminating in a finale in the east of the building. But these forms are no more present in the outer physical world than are melodies. These forms are walls that have come alive. Physical walls do not come alive, but etheric walls, spiritual walls do indeed come alive.

The art of sculptural relief—the 'living' wall

It would take a long time to explain why the art of sculptural relief only now assumes its true meaning, but I will give you just an indication of what I really have in mind. An eminent contemporary artist has said some clever things about the art of the relief.[5] He explains his conception of it thus: 'To make this quite clear, think of two panes of glass standing parallel to one another with a shape between them.' Seen in section it would look like this; you look through the glass walls in the direction of the arrow and see the shape between them.

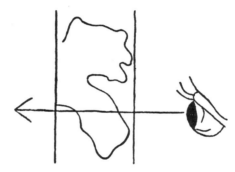

The shape is parallel to the glass walls and touches them at its highest points. 'The shape therefore occupies a space of even depth since its parts are arranged within the limits of this depth. Seen from the front through the pane of glass, on the one hand the shape represents a recognizable two-dimensional picture, and on the other hand an assumption of the amount of space it occupies is made easy even if the shape is complicated. The shape exists within a flat layer of even depth and all its forms spread out within this layer...'

What does all this mean? It means that the author is trying to form a conception of what a relief really is. But he is taking the eye as his starting point and trying to show that a relief comes about if you imagine it against a back wall made of glass and bounded by another wall of glass in front. Unlike Hildebrand's conception using glass walls, our conception of the relief is of something alive. We want to show how a relief is alive, for it has no meaning if it is simply a shape attached to a wall. It is only meaningful if it gives a sense of the wall itself being alive and giving birth to the shape.

There is a relief in existence which is full of meaning, only we cannot normally see it. It is a relief based on the right concepts: the surface of the wall reveals what it depicts. This relief is the surface of the earth itself, including the plant cover. In order to study it properly, however, we would have to step out into space and look back at its surface from there. The earth is the living surface that brings forth shapes. This is what our relief is to be like, giving us a clear sense that the wall is alive, just as we know that the earth is alive and can bring forth the plant world from its depths. Then we shall have achieved a genuine art of relief. To do more than this would be to sin against the essential nature of the relief. Looking down at the great relief of the earth we see people and animals moving upon it, but they do not belong to the relief. Of course we could include them in the relief, since the arts can be developed in all directions, but in essence it would then no longer be a pure art of relief.

Through the forms in its interior our building must speak in the language of the gods. Think for a moment of human beings living on the actual surface of the earth. We need not even draw on our spiritual science but can simply turn to the legend of Paradise. If human beings had remained in Paradise they would have looked from outside upon the wonderful relief of the earth with its flora. Instead, they were transplanted down to the earth where they now live within the relief without being able to see it from outside. They have departed from Paradise and the speech of the gods cannot reach them because the speech of the earth is louder and drowns it. If we pay heed to the organs of the gods which they themselves created when, as Elohim, they gave the earth to man, if we pay heed to the etheric forms of the plants and mould our walls in accordance with them, then—just as nature created the larynx in human beings in order that they might speak—we are indeed creating larynxes through which the gods may speak to us. When we listen attentively to the forms in our walls which are larynxes for the gods, we are seeking the way back to Paradise.

The smaller and the larger cupola

I will speak about painting in another lecture,[6] but today I want to dwell on the special kind of relief and sculpture to which the building we are inaugurating today is to be initially devoted. We have endeavoured to gain a sense of how a relief may become an organ of speech for the gods, and on some future occasion we will speak of how colours must become soul organs for the gods. Our age has very little understanding for the kind of conceptions that must inspire us if we are really to fulfill our task in the creation of our Goetheanum building.

We have seen how the Greek temple was the dwelling place of the god, and the Christian church the enclosure around the congregation seeking union with their god. What, then, is our building to be? Its fundamental character is revealed even in its ground plan and in its domed shape.

It has two sections, and the architectural forms of both are equally important, unlike the Christian church, where a difference is made between the chancel for the altar and the nave for the congregation. The difference in size simply signifies that in the large cupola the physical aspect is paramount, while in the smaller one we have tried to make the spiritual aspect predominant. The very form expresses aspiration to the spirit. Every single detail must express this aspiration to the spirit, inasmuch as we are striving to create an organ for the speech of the gods.

The architecture of love

I have said that those who really understand our building fully will set aside lying and wrongdoing, and that the building can become a 'lawgiver'. The truth of this can be studied in the individual forms. In a number of places in the architraves and the other forms you will find this specific feature [*drawing begins*].[7] Nowhere is it without meaning. Just as no part of the larynx is without meaning and no words would emerge if the larynx did not have the right form in the right place, so if you make a hollow shape here in the building, with a projection above it resembling eaves, this is an exact expression of the fact that this building must be filled with the feelings of those whose hearts stream together in love.

Nothing in this architecture is there for its own sake alone. One form leads over into another; or, if the forms have a threefold character, the middle part is the bridge between the other two. Here, in rough, are the forms of doors and windows:

Whereas forms in sculpture live in three dimensions, the relief is an overcoming of the two-dimensional surface so that it can begin to include the third dimension. We do not discover this by merely taking the viewpoint of an observer or spectator; we realize it when we gain a living sense of how the earth allows the plants to grow out of itself.

Colour and the soul of the universe

When I come to speak about painting we shall begin to understand the connection between colour and the inner element of soul in the universe. There would be no sense in painting with colours if colour were not something quite different from what physics considers it to be. Colour as the speech of the soul of nature, or of the soul of the universe, will be the subject of a later lecture.

The stained and engraved glass windows

I now want to indicate how our glass windows are to unite outside with inside.[8] Each window will be of one colour, but there will be different colours at different places, expressing the way the interplay between outside and inside must have a spiritual harmony. Within each monochrome window there will be thicker and thinner parts, parts where the physical substance is thicker, more solid, and parts where it is thinner. More light will shine in through the thinner parts and less through the thicker ones, which will thus yield darker shades. The interplay between spirit and matter will be sensed in what the windows express; and the whole of the interior surface will strive to be an organ for the speech of the gods. The larynx makes it possible for human beings to speak, and in the same way we shall sense that the whole shaping in relief of our building's interior is an organ with which the gods can speak to us from all directions of the universe. Everywhere there are speech organs of the gods.

What are we aiming for in seeking to make our walls permeable, in seeking to shape them in such a way that they negate themselves so that we can find a way of passing through them by making them into organs of speech for the gods? Our aim is none other than to show that we are searching for the path to the spirit by breaking through our walls and letting the gods use them as organs of speech. When we look at our windows they will tell us in the light and dark shading of their colours: 'Find thus, O Man, the path to the spirit!'

We shall see how the soul is related to the spiritual world when, in sleep at night, it lives outside the body. We shall see the way the disembodied soul is related to the spiritual world between death and a new birth. The windows will show us how human beings approaching the threshold of the spiritual world become aware of the abyss.[9] The stations on the path to the spiritual world will be revealed; they will arise like shapes of light, shining in from the western side and revealing to us the mysteries of initiation. We are trying to create walls, the forms of which make the walls themselves seem to dissolve. The pictures in the windows must show us how we are 'breaking through' the walls; they must show us the beings we shall encounter when we search for the path to the spiritual worlds or when we tread it unconsciously; they must show us the attitude we ought to have towards the spiritual worlds.

Living walls: from inner repose to inner activity

In earlier times people built the Greek temple as a dwelling place for the god. Later on they built a dwelling place for the congregation seeking union with their god. Both were intended to enclose what was within and exclude what lived outside. Our building will not exclude. Its walls must live and express the truth in their reliefs. The reliefs must express the experience we would have had of the living relief of the plant world if we had not been driven out of Paradise. We would have seen the living relief to which the earth gives birth in the forms of plants; we would have seen what emerges from the geological structures of the mountains, which are only bare where it is right and proper for them to be bare. Sitting there inside our building we must feel that we can be at rest and that then the gods can speak to us. But when the moment comes for us to move on from this state of repose, in which the gods speak to us, to a sense that we ourselves want to become inwardly active in finding the path to the gods, then we have to break through the wall. When this happens we must know what we have to do once we are within the spiritual world. So when we break through the walls the windows must be there to show our soul how to move towards the path that leads to the places from which came the speech brought to us by the forms of the walls. Our feeling must be that sitting here we are surrounded by the organs of speech of the spiritual world. We must want to learn how to understand the language spoken by the forms in such a way that we understand it with our hearts and not through merely intellectual interpretations.

Those who want to explain the 'meaning' of these forms are on the wrong track, as are those who interpret ancient myths and legends as symbols and allegories on the assumption that they are thus advancing the cause of anthroposophy. Someone trying to interpret myths and legends, and similarly the forms of our building, may be clever and ingenious, but this is the equivalent of looking under the chin to find an interpretation of the larynx. We understand the speech of the gods by learning how to listen with

The First Goetheanum, west elevation

our hearts, not by giving symbolic or allegorical meanings either to myths and legends or to our artistic forms. We must learn to sense how the spiritual world speaks to us. When this has become a living perception of what the soul must do if it is to find the way to those regions from which the speech of the gods proceeds, we shall turn our eyes to where the walls are pierced by the windows. There we shall be shown what lives in the human being who consciously or unconsciously treads the path from the physical to the spiritual world.

The holy mood necessary to create the larynx of the gods

With this let me conclude the heartfelt considerations I wanted to share with you today, as we hand over this building to the charge and careful work of our friend Rychter and his colleagues. May they feel, as they receive it, the sacred nature of their task, of which I have just spoken. Up there on the hill in our main building we are still working on the organs of speech which we want to create for the spirit, so that those who take their seats there will discover that the gods can speak to us through the medium of such organs. Once this has happened we must engender within us the sacred longing to find the path to the place where these spirits dwell. What Rychter and his colleagues will create here in this building will be carried up the hill and placed in the openings that will be left in the walls. These creations will move the souls of those who gather together up there on the hill and show them the path leading to the spirit.

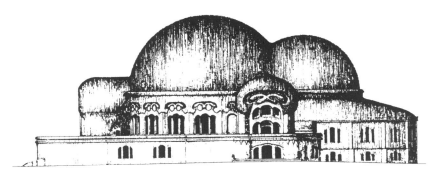

The First Goetheanum, south elevation

May this holy mood pervade this building; may every stroke of the cutter on the glass be carried out with the feeling: 'I am shaping something for the souls listening up there on the hill, something that will lead them out through space into the realms of spirit. My creations must make those souls' perceptions so living that the shadings in the coloured glass will show the way to that place from which the spiritual worlds speak through the interior forms of the building.' The difficulties may be very great; indeed there may be only partial success in many cases and in other cases total failure, but the attitude I have described will be an unfailing help if it can prevail here in these studios.

I did not intend to speak this evening about all kinds of things that might make art more intelligible. I have spoken as I have because I pray that something of what I feel may flow from my heart into yours. I want your hearts to be alive with a vibrant sense of the holiness of this work for our building. We dedicate this place of work most fitly if, as we leave its doors, we concentrate with all the forces of our hearts on love for the world of man and of spirit, so that the way to the spirit may be found by what is accomplished here—the spirit through which peace and harmony can flow among human beings on earth. If all our labours are made living by the spirit on whom I call here this evening, if all the work on this hill is filled with the spirit of love—which is at the same time the spirit of true art—then from our building there will flow out over the earth the spirit of peace, the spirit of harmony, the spirit of love. There will then be a chance for the work on this hill to find successors, so that many such centres of earthly and spiritual peace and harmony and love may spring up in the world. Let us seize hold of the living nature of our work in this mood of peace and loving harmony, so that our labours may flow from the spirit of life itself. There have been dwelling places for the gods and there have been sanctuaries for the congregation. Let there now be an organ of speech for the spirit and a sign pointing the way to the spirit. The god dwelt in the Greek temple, and the congregation can dwell in Romanesque or Gothic churches. Now let the world of spirit speak through the building of the future. We have seen the house of earthly forces and forms arise and pass away in the course of human evolution; we have seen the house of the union of human souls arise and pass away in the spiritual evolution of the earth. Now let us build the house of speech, the house whose walls all live and speak; let us build it out of our love for true art and thus out of our love for true spirituality and for all mankind.

The First Goetheanum, the fifth and sixth capital hoisted into place, 15 May 1914

A NEW CONCEPTION OF ARCHITECTURE
The astral body as a fully trained geometrician

Lecture Three, Dornach, 28 June 1914

From the Greek temple, via the early Christian basilica to the
Gothic church

As our building continues to grow it will be a good thing for us to
feel our way more and more into its meaning. We made a beginning in the two previous lectures, and we will try as far as we can to
continue our considerations so that we may unite with what is to
be accomplished here.

   In the first place I should like to remind you of a point I made
when we dedicated the studio where work is now proceeding on
the engraved windows.[1] I was referring to the evolution of architectural concepts, and I will very briefly recapitulate what was
anyway only an outline.

   I said of the Greek temple that it was a part of the surrounding
countryside, so that the countryside was at one with it. It stood
there as the dwelling place of the god and needed to contain
nothing but the god's spiritual presence and physical image. In
essence, the temple and its forms represented the fact that all the
people, engaged in their daily pursuits in the surrounding countryside, knew that they were not alone with the earth but also
united with the spiritual world. The temple standing there like an
altar in the landscape was a symbol of the fact that human beings
living on the earth were also united with the spiritual world.

We then saw how architectural concepts progressed to a time when Christian architecture separated off the building from the surrounding countryside. Everyday life and the more exalted mood in which people raised themselves to the spirit became two different things. The Christian church was no longer at one with the landscape. In serving the spirit it separated itself from the countryside, as though saying that human beings must leave the affairs of daily life in order to rise to the spirit; they must repair for a time to a place set apart and there be united with the spirit. The Christian church could no longer be what Greek and also Roman buildings had been. In itself it became a duality, a house for the congregation with a separate part for the altar and the priests. Human beings stepped outside the affairs of everyday life and entered the precinct where they could lift up their eyes to the spirit which came towards them from the chancel where the altar stood.

This evolution in architectural thought naturally implies the transformation of the ancient Greek form of building—which was derived purely from the interplay of static and dynamic factors of space and gravity—into a form corresponding to the idea of the congregation being set apart.

In the Gothic cathedral we have a still later concept of architecture. People not only brought their own selves into the church but also their individual craftsmanship: this expresses itself in the forms of Gothic architecture. The work of the craftsmen which surrounds us there can be experienced as a unity with the architectural forms, like folded hands raised in prayer to the spirit.

The building for our time

The point I made before was that another real advance in architectural conception must be achieved in our time; and that this will only be possible if the search for the spirit, which became increasingly apparent from the period of Greek architecture onwards to the Gothic conception, can gradually be transformed into a complete union with the spirit. This means that a building which is now to be dedicated to life in union with the spirit must in its very forms express an intimate correspondence with the spiritual world. By not explaining this in abstraction but grasping it instead with our whole life of feeling and soul, we could say that

The First Goetheanum, west aspect of the north wing

everything entering into and living in our soul through spiritual science is the very life in the forms we are creating. The spirit is experienced as free, having now descended to mankind.

The Greeks placed the temple into the countryside like an altar. But the future—and also the present, in so far as we are working out of the future in our building—places the spirit itself, and all that it expresses, into the landscape. What the spirit expresses in its forms is of course a kind of speaking, something that speaks to human beings today. For this to come about, we must endeavour to comprehend the spirit in the forms it generates. In order to understand the Greek temple, we tried, last time, to grasp the purely physical qualities of space and of gravity. But the spirit does not only work according to the laws of mechanics and dynamics, nor does it reveal itself solely in terms of space and the forces active in the structure. The spirit lives, and hence it must be expressed in our building in a living way, a truly living way. We shall not understand this any better if we begin to interpret the spirit symbolically. The only way is to feel that the forms are alive, that they are organs for what is spoken by the spiritual world.

To feel a circle is to feel our ego

Can forms speak out of the spiritual world? They can indeed, and they can express many things. Take a concept that is specially close to us, being on the one hand the expression of the highest, while on the other hand, in its luciferic aspect,[2] it is submerged in the lowest. Take the concept of the ego, the concept of the self.

We do not as yet attach anything particularly significant to the expression 'I', or 'self'. Many epochs will have to run their course in human history before a fully conscious mental image can arise in the soul when the word 'I' or 'self' is uttered. But there is a form we can make through which egohood or selfhood can be sensed. When we pass from having a purely mathematical conception of a form to really feeling what a form is, a perfect circle will give us a sense of egohood, of selfhood.[3] To feel a circle means to feel selfhood. To feel a circle in a plane, or a sphere in space, is to feel the self, the ego. Once you have grasped this you will readily follow the rest. When a human being who is truly alive to what he feels is confronted with a circle and in consequence feels a sense of ego, of self, arising in his soul, when even a part of the circle or a fragment of a sphere rouses in him a sense of independence in his own self, then he is learning to live in forms. Those whose feelings are truly alive are good at living in forms. If you bear this in mind you will find it easy to understand what follows from it.

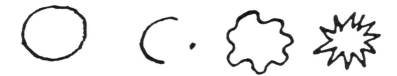

The first circle I have drawn here has an unbroken line. It can be varied by drawing a wavy line or by making it jagged. In each case it is still a circle, but what do the different forms mean? The second signifies that the self or ego has entered into a relationship with its environment. The simple circle makes us feel that the rest of the world is not there and only what is enclosed within the circle exists. The second circle does not make it seem as though what it encloses is all alone in the world. The wavy line expresses a conflict, an interplay with the environment. Someone who has a living sense for what the forms are saying will feel in regard to the second circle that the inside is stronger than what is outside, whereas in the case of the third circle such a person will feel that the outside is stronger and has forced its way towards the inside.

If we now enter a building and perceive fragments of circles or rounded surfaces with variations of this kind, we shall feel, in the case of jagged surfaces, that what is outside has been stronger, while in the case of undulating surfaces we shall sense that the inside has been the victor. Our soul begins to live with the forms. We do not merely look at them, but our soul has the living, surging feeling of victory or encroachment, overcoming or being vanquished. Our soul comes alive and begins to live in the forms. This union with form, this living in form, is the very essence of true artistic feeling.

The architecture of inner movement

We can go further still, by drawing a more complicated variation. Here the form is moving in a particular direction and becomes action. When we live in this form we have the feeling that it moves and is advancing. The form itself is characteristic of movement.

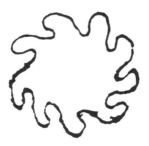

I have here made a simple sketch of something that will appear in a complicated form in our building, and yet you will find that the result is entirely homogeneous. Going from the western entrance through the auditorium towards the stage, you will find that all the forms in the interior evoke the feeling that everything is proceeding from west to east. This is expressed by the forms. Entering the building from the west you will have the idea in your feelings that you are being borne along in a carriage towards the spiritual east. The very essence and meaning of these variations in the sculptured surfaces is that they do not merely envelop us like dead, dynamic or mechanical forms; we seem to enter a vehicle, a carriage that bears us onwards. In a spiritual sense we shall not be at rest in our building; we shall be led ever onwards.

You will now realize that the fundamental character of the forms here is quite different from that of the forms in the three historical stages of architectural conception I described earlier. Hitherto the concept of architecture has been concerned with the qualities of lifeless, mechanical rest. Now, however, the concept of architecture becomes a concept of speaking, of moving inwardly, of being drawn along by something. This is one side of what is new in our concept of architecture. The basic shape, however, has to correspond to this, and we must now ask how it is achieved.

We have already pointed out that the circle or sphere is the closest to us because it engenders the impression of the self, the ego. This is because a simple sphere or circle is, of all forms, the most easily perceptible. It is an absolutely easy matter to define a circle. All you need is the familiar idea that everything is equidistant from the central point. Picture a whole lot of points at an equal distance from the centre and you have a sphere or a circle. It is the easiest of all thought processes, and thus the circle is the least mysterious of all forms. This also corresponds with external reality, for the self in every living creature, from the simplest cell to the complex human being, gives us the most ordinary, everyday impression, just as a sphere or circle gives us the most ordinary impression.

Behind all this there is, however, something much more profound, and I now want you to follow me in a thought that will lead those who really understand it to great depths.

The ellipse—the curve of addition

An ellipse is a form that is somewhat more complicated than a circle.[4] Here is the ellipse we are all used to seeing. It need not be exact so long as it is generally recognizable. Passing from the circle to the ellipse we find ourselves with a thought that is no longer quite so simple. Although the ellipse lacks the evenness of the circle, it nevertheless has a regular shape. For politeness sake we will assume that you all know a little geometry, though you may have forgotten some of it, but those who have studied geometry will find it easier to understand the ideas I am about to explain.

An ellipse is a regular form. While the circle relates to a single point, the ellipse relates to two. The line segments between any point of the ellipse and the two foci will naturally differ in length, but the sum of these two lengths will be constant.

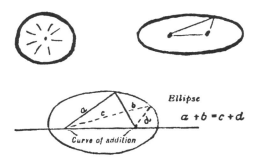

Ellipse

$$a + b = c + d$$

Curve of addition

You can add the distance of each point from these two foci and you will always get the same length. In the case of the circle this is so simple that there is no need for any mental process. In the case of the ellipse, however, we must make an addition. All lines to the centre of a circle are equal, but in the ellipse we have to make an addition.

The astral body is a geometrician

You might now wish to point out that you do not, in fact, do any adding up when you see an ellipse. This is true, but your astral body does; what the geometrician does consciously the astral body does unconsciously, for it is a fully-trained geometrician. You have no idea of all of the knowledge that is contained in your astral body. In it you are an immensely learned geometrician, only of course the geometry you know in your astral body can only be brought into consciousness with considerable effort. Everything is present down there in your astral body, and if those who teach geometry could instead utilize a pump they would no longer have any need for their usual teaching methods. The knowledge would well up of its own accord. We add, then, the two distances from the foci and always get the same result. What does it really mean when we find beauty in an ellipse? It means that our astral body is adding up and the sum total is always the same. Imagine yourself adding up without knowing it and every time getting the same answer. You feel pleased. From this point you get the same result, and then from that one again, and this fills you with delight. This is the living experience of the ellipse.

In the case of the circle there is no such feeling of delight, for the circle is so immediately obvious. The ellipse causes us greater pleasure because there we have to be inwardly active. The more we are inwardly active, the greater the pleasure we experience. People find it so difficult to realize that the human being, in his inner being, craves for activity. It is only in his conscious life that he wants to be lazy. The astral body is not only wiser, but also more industrious and would like to be active all the time.

The hyperbola—the curve of subtraction

Let us turn to another curve, one that consists of two portions. Those of you who have studied geometry will know that the hyperbola consists of two symmetrical branches.[5] It also has two foci, situated approximately here [*see drawing*]. Again we can draw lines to these two points. The strange thing is that instead of adding we now subtract. We always get the same result by subtracting the lesser from the greater. Our astral body subtracts and is pleased that the difference is always the same. In this inner feeling of two things being equal the astral body experiences how the hyperbola comes into being.

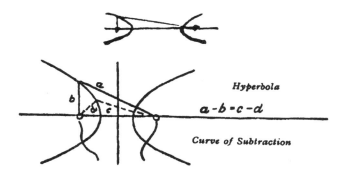

Hyperbola

$a - b = c - d$

Curve of Subtraction

The lemniscate—the curve of multiplication

We are unconscious calculators, and by means of subconscious calculation we create regularity of form. We add and subtract, and we can also multiply.[6] Again we have two points, and by multiplying a by b and c by d we again arrive at a curve that resembles an ellipse although it is not the same. This curve [I] contains an inner process of multiplication and is rather mysterious. A circle is perfectly simple, an ellipse somewhat more complicated and a hyperbola more complicated still, since most people do not realize that it is in fact one curve, although it looks like two. This next curve is mysterious in a different way because, depending on the result of the multiplication, it changes into this curious shape [II]. This multiplication curve, the lemniscate, is the very curve that plays such an important part in occult investigations. It can even go so far as to change into this shape [III].

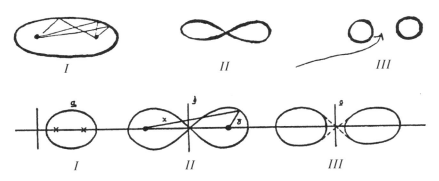

Again this looks like two curves although inwardly they are one, and when our astral body senses that they are one we know that this form [III] is merely a special case of this one [II]. But now imagine that the crossing point disappears together [III] with the curve and then it reappears in the physical world once more. It disappears again and then reappears again. It is one curve that keeps disappearing. You could say that this multiplication curve has three different forms.

The circle—the curve of division

We have so far looked at a curve arising from addition, one arising from subtraction, and another arising from multiplication. So you might expect there to be a curve arising from division as well. It would be a matter of dividing two distances instead of adding, subtracting or multiplying them. It would have to be possible for our astral body to determine two points and also other points. If it were to divide the longer line segment by the shorter one, and here the longer by the shorter, and so on, a curve would result: which is this circle.[7] All the points are chosen so that their distances from these two points result in the same answer when they are divided.

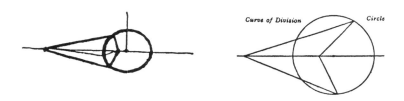

By adding we arrive at the ellipse, by subtracting we arrive at the hyperbola, by multiplying we arrive at the Cassini curve, the lemniscate, and by dividing we arrive at the circle.

We have now come to something very remarkable indeed. When we really try to penetrate them fully, the depths of nature rise up before our soul in all their wonder. A circle at first appears to be an entirely simple matter, and then we discover it to be full of mystery.[8] One way of understanding it is by dividing in relation to two points; a circle comes about when the result is the same in each case. It is quite remarkable, being on the one hand so ordinary that it is easily comprehended, while on the other hand it is the result of occult division made conscious. It is the same in the case of the human self. The ordinary self is an everyday entity, while the higher self is something mysterious resting in the depths of our soul, a self that can only be found when we transcend its limits and pay heed to the world with which it is connected. The circle is the same whether we say that it is the simplest of all forms or that the product of division from two points is always equal. Within us we have the same duality: something that belongs to everyday life and is readily perceptible, and something that we only grasp when we go out into the whole universe, conceiving of this entity as the most complicated product of the great cosmic struggle where Ahriman and Lucifer carry out the division in relation to which our own higher self has to maintain itself as the quotient if it is to come to expression.[9]

Portions of ellipse and of hyperbola, and also of the lemniscate, will be found everywhere in our building, and your astral body will have plenty of opportunity to make these calculations. Mention of one instance will suffice. When people in our building look up to the gallery where the organ and choir will be, their souls will be able to carry out multiplications. Though they may not do so consciously, they will feel it in their depths because the curve of the structure around the organ will call for multiplication. The same curve will be found in many other places as well.

Path from the lower to the higher self

After what I have now told you about the twofold significance of the circle you will be able to realize, when you enter the building from the west and feel yourselves surrounded by the circular structure, and by the dome above, that here is the image of the human self. But the smaller interior to the east will not at first sight be so intelligible. The smaller structure will seem to be full of mystery because, although its form is also circular, it must be conceived of as the result of a process of division, and it only outwardly resembles the larger space. There are two circles, but the one corresponds to the life of everyday while the other is connected with the whole cosmos. We bear within us a lower self and a higher self, yet both are one. Thus our building had to be a twofold structure. Its form expresses the dual nature of man—not in any symbolical sense but because the form is as it is. When the curtain in front of the stage is open we shall sense an image of the human being not only as he is in everyday life, but as complete being. Because the forms express a movement from west to east, they directly express the path of the lower to the higher self.

Everything I have been telling you can be felt in the forms. A building of this kind reveals how nature's spiritual forms and also the higher spiritual world can be expressed in a manner befitting both nature and spirit. Those who try to think out all kinds of ingenious interpretations will fail to understand our building, for it

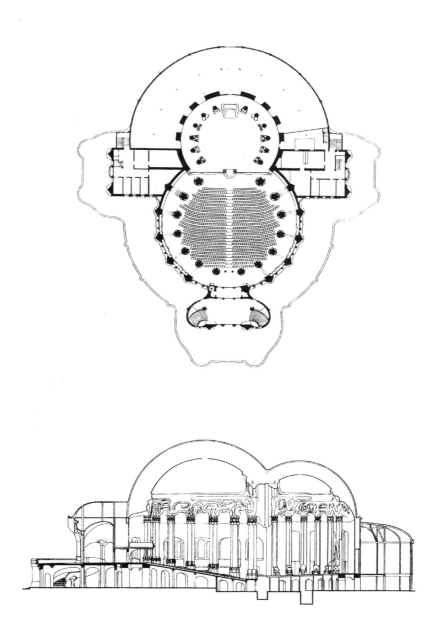

The First Goetheanum, ground plan and west/east section

can only be comprehended by a living sense of how its forms come into being and of what their essence is. That is why I do not want to describe it in pictures. I want to tell you how it developed and how spirit itself became form and movement and flowed into our building. Someone looking at the interior of our building might be tempted to speculate: 'Two cupolas, two circular structures; lower self, higher self—a unity.' This could be a neat interpretation, but it would be of no more value than to say that Maria and Thomasius in the Mystery Dramas are really one and the same being. It is mere speculation, for it results in an abstraction, whereas the unity lies in the living process of becoming. Of course the living powers of becoming can produce both Maria and Thomasius, but only as the result of differentiation. In sameness the true occultist will always seek for diversity, for wanting to derive sameness from diversity would be false occultism. Hence the example of the circle. The circle is the simplest thing, where the points are all equidistant from the centre; but it is also the result of the process of division. It is a unity in the outer world but something complex in the spiritual world.

   This is all I have to say on this for the moment. On another occasion I shall speak about the building itself, but for the moment let us turn to another aspect.

Our seven pairs of 'life pillars'

As we appear on earth we are highly complex.[10] When we first arrive we cannot stand upright. We crawl; indeed, at first we cannot even do that. Then gradually we master the forces that allow us to become upright. A diagram will help us to explore what is involved. Here is the earth [*drawing begins*]. First we live in the horizontal; subsequently we stand up and become vertical. We achieve this vertical stance out of our own human nature, but we have the help of all the hierarchies throughout our life. What helps us to stand up and to walk are the forces that rise up from the earth and work towards the expanse of the cosmos. Here are these earthly forces [*see drawing*]. Today physicists speak only of physical forces of attraction and gravity. The earth, however, is not merely a physical body but a being of spirit and soul, and when, as little children, we raise ourselves to the upright position and walk, we are uniting ourselves with the forces of will rising up out of the earth. This earth-will permeates our being; we allow it to flow through us, we place ourselves upright—in the direction of the earth-will, making it our ally. In opposition to the earth-will, however, there is another will that presses in from all directions of the cosmos. Although we are unaware of it, forces are working in from all sides as we raise ourselves to the upright position. We collide with these forces that are pouring in from outside as we stand up.

This situation no longer has any particular significance here on earth, but during the period of ancient Moon it was immensely significant. The conditions at that time were such that from our earliest childhood we had a different orientation from that of the present time, in that we had to place ourselves within the direction of the moon-will. As a result of this we acquired the first beginnings of our cranium. Nowadays this is something we inherit, but at the time of ancient Moon it was a question of acquiring it. We had to push away the will forces coming from outside—rather as a locomotive pushes away snow—compressing our soft cranium so that it became hard. Today this is something we inherit. We no longer have to create the bones of our skull. But we do still create them in our ether body, for as we rise to the upright position there is a densification in the head resulting from the battle between the forces streaming out from the earth and those streaming in from all around.

From this we can go on to say that in observing the ether body we still find that with both legs we set up vertical lines with which we work against the forces coming in from outside. We can then observe the resulting densification that creates this form [*see drawing*]. We stand. Our physical legs go up as far as our torso,

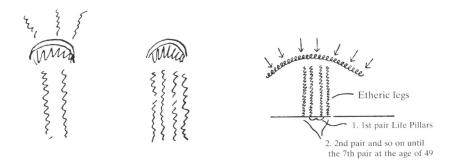

Etheric legs

1. 1st pair Life Pillars

2. 2nd pair and so on until
the 7th pair at the age of 49

but our etheric legs go up further. Thus the ether body of our head is densified, and so even today our densified etheric head arises through the formation of the brain. This does not only take place in childhood; it continues as we pass through seven periods of life. From the first to the seventh year, from the seventh to the fourteenth, and so on, more and more vertical lines of varied forces come into being. By the time we have become fully mature human beings at the respectable age of fifty, we have added pair after pair to those first strong pillars which we built up during our first seven years. They appear in the ether body in different colours. With every pair of what I will call 'life pillars' we strengthen our etheric cranium. At the end of our first seven years the first pair is completed, at fourteen the second, at twenty-one the third, until finally at forty-nine the seventh pair is there. With every pair of these life pillars we bear our etheric cranium more securely.

Need you do more than imagine the way we human beings go through life raising up within ourselves every seven years differently-shaped pairs of pillars that bear our cranium? Surely not! Once you have taken this in you will have acquired a living understanding of the inner form of the larger round section of our building. Entering from the west you find that up to the first pair of columns it is like the human being developing during our first seven years, and that up to the second pair it is like the development from our seventh to our fourteenth year, and then to twenty-one, and so on. Around you, you continue to have the cranium. Here, cast into form, is the human being as we really are, as we live in our ether body.

*The First
Goetheanum—interior
looking east on to stage*

*Four steps in earthly evolution: Greek, early Christian, Gothic, and
our time*

It is in this way that Gothic architecture will be transformed into
the architecture of spiritual science. In Gothic times people prayed:
'O Father of the universe, may we be united with Thee, in Thy
Spirit.' Gothic architecture expresses this. Those who can bring
themselves to accept what is granted in answer to this prayer, and
who truly understand the living development of spiritual science,
will be able to solve the riddle of human beings and our evolution.
As the forms in our architecture endeavour to unite with the
spirit—though they express only the endeavour as yet—so we will
begin to feel that we have become spiritualized human beings
within a building that clearly expresses the inner nature of the
human being, comprehending ourselves in our inner living being.

'We dwell in the open countryside, and the spirit is amongst us.'
So speaks the idea of Greek architecture.

'While we tarry in the sanctuary the spirit comes to us.' So speaks the idea of early Christian architecture.

'We tarry in the church, and our soul is uplifted as we raise ourselves in anticipation to the spirit.' So speaks the idea of Gothic architecture.

'We enter with reverence into the spirit in order that we may become one with the spirit that is poured out in forms around us, because the Spirits of Form are around us, and these forms move because the Spirits of Movement stand behind the Spirits of Form.' So speaks the idea of the new architecture!

Thus the mode of existence changes through the stages of earthly evolution and it is the human being's task to understand its inner sense and meaning. We only keep pace with evolution when we endeavour, in every epoch, to experience what the spiritual world bestows in that epoch.

Why do we as souls pass through different, successive incarnations? It is not in order to experience the same things over and over again; not in order to experience the Renaissance and then again the Renaissance, but in order to assimilate into our souls whatever is new in all that the spiritual world pours forth. In this sense we are now at a turning point in human evolution—in the sphere of art as well as other spheres of cultural life—where the spirit is clearly setting us new riddles. Just as the Renaissance was a time when people strove to find their new direction by referring to what had existed in the past, so we are now in a similar position with regard to our knowledge and perception of the universe. What the modern age has yielded since the sixteenth century has been a preparation for precisely this experience of the universe in its forms and movements that now appear as riddles before us.

This is all for today. In another lecture I will try to approach questions of a still more intimate character, ones relating to the living soul of nature in connection with colour and painting.

THE AESTHETIC LAWS OF FORM
Consciously penetrating the forms and colours of the spiritual sea of the cosmos as a precondition for true art

Lecture Four, Dornach, 5 July 1914

Architectural forms derived from the path of knowledge

In the last lecture we spoke of the spirit that is to pervade the forms in our building, and from all that was said you will have gathered that these forms are neither imitations of the external, physical world nor are they based on haphazard theories. You will have sensed that they have been derived from the spiritual world of which human beings are a part and to which human beings may hope to win through on spiritual science's path of knowledge. I mentioned the way in which human life, from the spiritual-scientific point of view, is measured in seven-year periods, and showed that during each such period a new pair of supports is gained, so that at the age of about fifty, after seven times seven periods have elapsed, the human being possesses seven such pairs of supports.

Entering our building from the west, we come upon the first two columns and find in them an expression of the 'life-supports' we have created within ourselves by the end of our first seven years. In the second pair of columns we discover what we acquire during the course of the second seven-year period, and so on. Although the human being creates these supports one within the other, here in the space of our building they appear in sequence. As you walk through this space from west to east there is something to your left and to your right that gives you a sense of what takes place during the course of a human being's life. Thus you discover firmly-established universal laws to which the human being is subject, laws which are infinitely more profound than those commonly known as the laws of nature. It is in accordance with these profound universal laws that the forms in our building have been created.

Why the seven woods in the Goetheanum?

It would be going too far for us now to study every detail from this point of view, but it could be done. In the present climate, in which there is no knowledge of spiritual science, it will be difficult for people to grasp these deeper laws underlying all existence, so it is understandable if they ask, for example, why the columns are made from different woods. There is certainly no allegorical or symbolic reason, and anyone asking the question merely shows that life has afforded him or her no opportunity to wonder about profounder universal laws. We can only reply with another question: 'Why not use only A-strings on a violin?' Thinking it is fine to string a violin with four A-strings is no different from enquiring— quite naïvely, as a result of superficial knowledge—why the columns are made of different woods.

Macrocosm and microcosm as the basis for aesthetic laws

Since we shall often be meeting here we can take our time over these questions, gradually gaining a sense for what will assist our understanding. Therefore today I only want to approach something that can help us gain a feeling for the way the aesthetic laws of form are rooted on the one hand in the macrocosm and on the other in the microcosm of human nature. What we nowadays know as science will, before long, undergo an overwhelming expansion, and only then will understanding of the true and deeper laws of aesthetic form come about.

To give you a more concrete sense of what I mean let me show you a great fact of the macrocosm by means of a diagram that depicts sun, earth and moon, without taking their relative sizes and distances into account.

For the clairvoyant consciousness of the occult observer the spiritual reality of these three heavenly bodies fills the universe.

When the occult observer approaches them with his clairvoyant consciousness he finds that the whole universe is filled with the interweaving of their spiritual beings. As you know, all heavenly bodies are inhabited by spiritual beings who not only live there but also send forth their influences. Higher beings live there permanently, while subordinate beings are sent from one to another,

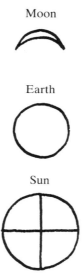

Moon

Earth

Sun

thus setting cosmic currents in motion. These currents are nothing less than the paths followed by elemental or higher beings from one heavenly body to another. Clairvoyant consciousness first sees what appear to be magnetic or electrical currents flowing through the cosmos from one heavenly body to another. More exact observation reveals a host, a stream, a swarm of spiritual beings journeying from one heavenly body to another.

Microcosmic example: circulation of spirit beings

Sun, earth and moon occupy a specific mutual relationship. They send their influences to one another, and it is about one particular kind of influence that I want to speak to you today. First I must divide up the sun to show how it appears to the occult observer when he directs his attention to these things. It is divided cross-wise into four portions or chambers.

There appears to be a current but the remarkable thing is that closer scrutiny reveals hosts of beings travelling back and forth. The stream of wandering beings passes from something like a chamber in the sun [I] to the earth, right into the earth, vitalizing it with solar essence—that is to say, with the spiritual force of the sun—and then returning to another chamber in the sun [III].

This is a cosmic reality, and there is more to come. Here is another current, a migration of hosts of spiritual beings flowing around and through the moon. They proceed from this sun chamber [IV] and they also flow round the other way into the moon. [*The two streams from chamber IV are drawn, passing through the moon and returning to chamber IV.*]

So far we see the activities of the inhabitants of three chambers of the sun [I, III and IV]. These beings [IV] stream from the fourth chamber in a double current to the moon, always returning to the fourth chamber. But now another current ensues because some do not go all the way to the moon but turn back towards the sun here [*the path from IV to II is drawn*].

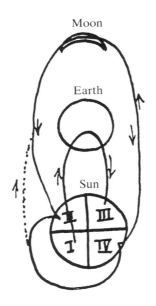

There is a kind of mirror image of this figure in the cosmos [*the movement from IV through the moon to II is drawn*], but we will leave this out of consideration for the moment.

I will now draw the diagram slightly differently with the cross in the sun turned a little.

It is the same situation as before, only the cross is turned and consequently the lines are a little different, but they emerge from and flow into the same chambers of the sun. [*To the previous*

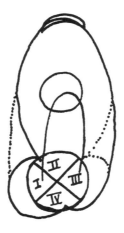

streams are added the mirror-image streams from chamber IV to II and from chamber IV through the moon to chamber II.] As you can see, this mirror-image would complete the figure that has come about and is seen as though engraved upon the cosmos. This mirror-image completes our diagram and makes it symmetrical. The whole thing shows us that for clairvoyant consciousness there is a marvellous configuration as though engraved upon the cosmos, representing the interplay between the forces of sun, moon and earth.

Microcosmic example: circulation of the blood

I will now change the diagram again and include the assumption that the beings which we are used to calling Ahriman and Lucifer have come into the picture,[1] bringing disorder in their train. I will make sun, moon and earth irregular in shape and now once more draw the connecting streams. The result is exactly the same as in the other diagrams, only somewhat distorted by Ahriman and Lucifer, and you will see that it shows the circulation of the blood in the human being. It is a sketch of the blood flowing from the left ventricle of the heart [II] through the brain on the one hand; and on the other through the rest of the body, returning as venous blood [*to the right auricle,* IV]. You also see the course of the small circulatory stream through the right ventricle [III] and lungs back again to the left auricle [I].

Thus we can read from the cosmos what the human being is as a microcosm, only it must be remembered that Ahriman and Lucifer have come upon him. Man is bound up with the cosmos; he truly expresses all the great cosmic connections. We need only add that the heart is the microcosm of the sun, the lungs the microcosm of the earth and its hierarchy of forces, and the brain the microcosm of the moon; then our diagram becomes an expression of immensely significant connections.

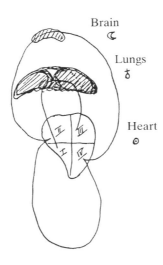

Our astral body as perceptive organ enthusing the soul

If a shape were to be made from this diagram, its very form, copied from the cosmos and expressed in an artistic motif, would give us a sense of a profound cosmic mystery. When a certain combination of lines underlies a shape of this kind—where perhaps only a few of these lines are expressed and the others drawn in quite another way—those who have real feeling, and not merely intellectual understanding, will perceive a cosmic mystery in the very form itself. They will sense that the form expresses a mystery, though they may not know its meaning. It is this that enthuses our soul and makes our heart beat faster when we look at certain shapes and forms. We cannot always be conscious of what lies behind them, but our astral body, our subconscious being, contains the mysteries of the cosmos and senses them in the depths just as it contains the secrets of mathematics, as I told you in the previous lecture. When we find something beautiful but do not quite know why, something is taking place within our astral body. We sense profound mysteries of the universe, and these are expressed in us not through thoughts and ideas but through a feeling that says: 'Ah, how beautiful is this form!' The reason we feel this as warmth pouring through our heart and soul is that if we were as conscious in our astral body as we are in our ego we would at that moment experience a deep moment of knowledge about the cosmos.

These things must help us to understand how art gradually came about in human evolution and to realize that, in the Goethean sense, true works of art manifest laws of nature more exalted than anything we can even remotely divine with our ordinary intellect.[2]

Primitive art and atavistic clairvoyance

We find an inkling of the truth of these things more especially when we go back to what modern opinion holds to be the 'primitive' art of earlier periods of human evolution. This is because in those ancient times a primitive, atavistic clairvoyance was a common attribute of humanity, so that people of those times created forms out of this clairvoyance. Many of the forms to be found in primitive art can only be understood when we realize that they were the outcome of this primordial clairvoyant consciousness. People experienced the content of their astral bodies as living movement. They tried to express it within themselves as a kind of noble dance which they then converted from Dionysian dancing to Apollonian drawing and painting (as I indicated in earlier lectures).[3] Hence arose the forms of early art which often seem to us merely primitive, but which in truth have sprung from a deeper understanding of the spiritual world imparted by the clairvoyance of those times.

In the case of genuine art it is perfectly apt to say that there can be no disputing about taste. You can work your way through to an understanding of how true art is founded on laws and forms that are every bit as certain as the laws of mathematics, based as they are on the deeper laws of existence. Art is a manifestation of higher natural laws that would never be revealed without art, and there is no disputing these higher laws.

Art forms that assist us in transcending our materialistic consciousness

If we regard this less as an idea that can be thought and more as a feeling, it can lead us to a sense of what happens to us when we take delight in forms that are truly artistic. We step out of ourselves and immerse our soul in cosmic realities that are outside us. Therefore it is not at all unnatural that in a building that belongs to the present and the future we should set out in full consciousness to create forms which will help human beings to conquer their consciousness of merely physical and material actuality, and to feel themselves extended out into the cosmos through the architecture, sculpture and all that this work of art may contain. Much will have to be done, however, so that this feeling will be able to penetrate into every sphere of art and be admitted by modern science.

Is animal colouring determined by natural selection?

Darwinism[4] and all that it brought in its train in the nineteenth century has rendered great service to the progress of human knowledge and culture, but it has also given rise to many one-sided conceptions, for instance in what it calls the law of natural selection. Knowledge of this law is very important, but to lay it down as a universal law is to be one-sided. A materialist who believes only in the physical world will maintain that we are no longer as simple-minded as our ancestors. This is because he does not believe that there were spiritual beings who originally endowed creatures with their practical adaptations to the environment. It was simply part of nature, he believes, that the fit and the unfit should have arisen haphazardly and that this then resulted in the struggle for the survival of the fittest in which the fit conquered and the unfit were exterminated. The well-adapted winners passed their traits on to their descendants so that eventually only the fit remained. Thus the law of cause and effect was applied to explain the survival of well-adapted species.

Take the example of an animal whose colouring merged with that of its environment, let's say the desert. Those who think in terms of cause and effect will maintain that this animal was well adapted because its enemies could not see it and therefore did not pursue it. It had an advantage over other animals whose colour differed from that of the sand, for they were attacked and destroyed and were thus at a disadvantage in the struggle for the survival of the fittest. The one, however, that happened to have the same colour as the sand survived and passed its characteristics on to future generations. The ones with different colours became extinct but the sand-coloured one survived in the process of natural selection.

This is a highly plausible train of thought and it has dominated people's minds for decades. In sandy places there are all kinds of small creatures whose colour is exactly that of the sand, and according to materialistic Darwinism they are supposed to have come into being in the manner just described. The fact of the matter is, however, that as soon as they show themselves their enemies pounce and eat them up to their hearts' content. The whole conception is based upon a train of reasoning that does not reckon with the actual facts. It is a fanciful idea rooted in materialism.

Animal colouring caused by the astral body

All these materialistic speculations and fancies will one day be replaced by true insight. Such insight may seem grotesque and paradoxical to many people even though, for instance, it will provide the real reason why the polar bear is white and not black or brown. The insight will arise that there is an astral nature, that every animal has an astral body and that soul processes have their seat in this astral body. Although the sand-coloured creatures of the desert have no ego of their own they have an astral body, primitive though it may be. An interplay arose between the astral body and the colour of the environment, and the effects produced by this interplay between the sandy colour of the environment and the astral body passed into the dimmer consciousness of the astral body and permeated the whole creature. When you come in here[5] you say: 'This is wood; I know that it is wood.' In the same way the animal lived in the sand while its astral body was filled with the colour of the sand. A consciousness that said 'sandy colour' flowed through its whole being, so that it took on the colour, saturated itself with the colour of its environment.

Its colour was, of course, modified by the struggle that arose between the immediate colour of the environment and the direct light of the sun. The effect of direct sunlight on the astral body was such that because of the nature of the soul something actually entered the astral body and then radiated out and filled the whole animal. In the colours of bird plumage and animal fur we will come to recognize the more mysterious result of the consciousness that arose in the interplay between the astral body and the environment. The living creature still lives and moves in the flowing sea of colour and identifies itself with this flowing essence of colour.

Human colouring due to climate

Humans also do this below the threshold of their ego, although in a higher sense; our life is bound up with this life of the flowing sea of colour. As human beings we have an advantage over animals in only one aspect, which I can do no more than hint at just now. Think of animals that swim under water without ever coming to the surface; they have adapted to what they take into themselves from the water. Others live above the water and are thus adapted to what exists above the surface. Instead of the water, think now of a flowing sea of colour and light. All the animals live within this sea of colour, below its surface, and hence they adjusted their outer covering primarily in accordance with this flowing colour and light.

Human beings, however, rose above the surface of the flowing sea of colour and light and so gained their ego consciousness. When the colouring of the skin was influenced, as in the different races, the influence was not the outcome of colour and light but of the conditions of temperature and climate. The reason why humming birds in a particular region are decked with such a variety of hues is quite different from the reason for the humans in the same region being clad in a black, African skin. The plumage of the humming bird is the result of colour and light, whereas the colour of human skin is the result of temperature and climate. This is because, in effect, the human being emerged with his ego above the surface of the sea of colour. It is only with his astral body that he interacted with the colour. To put it rather drastically, if humans had not emerged with their ego above the sea of colour, then country people living mainly in a green environment would have green skins, whereas the skin of city dwellers, interacting from the beginning with the drabness of their city, would have taken on the grey colour of their surroundings.

Colour gives rise to feelings

In a sense we, too, float with our astral body in the flowing sea of colour, but what our astral body absorbs from this sea of colour is taken up in a different way. We do not colour our hair, nor do we grow feathers coloured by what our astral body absorbs. Instead of this we have perceptions and feelings in connection with

The First Goetheanum—detail of ceiling painting by Rudolf Steiner above the stage: an angelic being with Slav people below

colours, without painting ourselves externally with them. Were we simply to absorb the green or blue or red into our astral body and diffuse them through our being, thus giving ourselves the colouring of our environment, we should have quite a different relationship to the world of colour than is actually the case. We do not, however, do this. We absorb the colours into our being in a spiritual sense, so that blue, for instance, becomes the expression of rest, or red the expression of all that is passionate and fiery. Because we reach out with our ego beyond the flowing sea of colour, it is changed for us into flowing perception or feeling. Here is proof that with regard to colour we float within the cosmos, so that when we see colour, even if it is only the colour of the natural world, we cannot help wanting to have aesthetic feelings about it and applying standards of beauty. This implies that we must learn to grow into colours, to live in them as though within our own element.[6]

One seldom finds this feeling for colour, even among people who think a great deal about art. Even Hildebrand,[7] an exceedingly good artist who has written an imaginative book on the subject of form in art, states that a picture cannot be painted with colour on its own. In his opinion the drawing comes first, and this leads on to the colour. He thinks that when he applies paint to a canvas he is simply looking at blue, perhaps, or red, that does not represent anything in particular. He believes that he has to draw a design before anything is depicted. This is, however, not correct. A surface covered with blue elicits an impression, a feeling of being taken into greater and ever greater depths, of being sucked into the remote distances of infinity. Blue invites you to go along with it, on and on. With red, on the other hand, you have the feeling that it is coming towards you or even attacking you.

This is putting it rather drastically, but the colours in the spectrum only reveal their characteristics when they come alive before our very eyes. Just as forms with clear contours express something definite, so do colours place before us something quite definite and differentiated. In the future the task of art will be to enable us to enter fully into these things. In what sense do I mean this? If we wish to understand in what sense, then we must first reach a clear picture of the real spirit of human evolution.

The objective effect of colours resulting from our evolution

Human evolution began with primitive, atavistic, clairvoyant consciousness. The human being journeyed through the various cultural epochs until in the Greco-Roman age his ego came to birth in the intellectual or mind-soul.[8] In the present age our ego is being drawn up into the consciousness soul, whence it will then gradually rise further into the spirit-self or manas.

In the ages preceding the birth of the ego into ego consciousness, art proceeded from direct inspiration which flowed into human beings from the spiritual world, and all the different forms in art were an expression of this enlivening impulse coming from the spiritual world. For example, going out as night fell and seeing the moon, human beings felt in their atavistic clairvoyance how the connection between their brain and the moon was being revealed to them, and how with their lungs they were inhaling what the earth had to tell them about their being; although the sun had set, they knew that it was being revealed in the pulsing beat of their heart. They felt, or rather they saw with the atavistic clairvoyance of those ancient times, how earth, sun and moon were interconnected. Spirits hovered up and down between sun and moon:

> Like heavenly forces rising and descending,
> Their golden urns reciprocally lending.[9]

Goethe's words describe this movement, just as human beings in ancient times wanted to express the movements that were going on. Something enters our hand when we sense the movement in the cosmos and this is how we express it in chalk, whether it is simple or as complicated as can be. [*Apparently this was demonstrated by Rudolf Steiner on the blackboard but no record survives.*]

Then came the age in human evolution when this old clairvoyance gradually passed away; more and more, human beings emerged into a condition in which they could only perceive the external world of the senses. Nothing more flowed into people from the spiritual world, so they had to resort to taking what they wanted to express from elsewhere. Originally every artistic impulse lived in the moving being within. What people felt about the world went straight into their hands and with their hands they sought to relive and then express what had flowed into them from the cosmos. These gestures then had to be remoulded into some kind of form. It was not a question of copying anything. All that lived and pulsated in humans, what grew into them out of the cosmos, what glowed and surged through them became art, without imitation. Their own flowing inner life guided their tools; the cosmos itself became active within them and guided their tools.

This ended when the ancient atavistic clairvoyance linking humans with the cosmos also ceased. Imitative art began when people no longer felt their tools being guided from within, when they no longer felt they wanted to find their way to the gods and approach the divine. When that was still the case a blaze of blue had met their gaze when they approached the gods, so they had expressed it in blue. And when an enemy approached, an alien being bearing down, red flared up. This was a direct experience, so there was no need for imitation. But when the atavistic connection with the cosmos ceased this was no longer the case. Imitative art began, reaching its culmination in sculpture in the Greco-Roman age and its culmination in painting around the beginning of the fifth post-Atlantean period.[10]

For those who have eyes to see, even external history would be able teach them the truth of these things. Ask yourselves why it was that the tribes coming down from northern or central Europe to mingle with the Greco-Roman peoples were for so long regarded by them as barbarians incapable of finding their way into art. It was because those Celtic, Germanic and Slav peoples still retained an earlier stage of consciousness. Their ego was not yet fully born and so they had no understanding of imitative art. They were latecomers from an earlier age. Therefore the significant elements of the art of the Middle Ages are not those arising from imitation. In studying the art of the Middle Ages we will discover that it is art which is not imitative that is of greatest significance. We will discover that the essence of medieval architecture and crafts arises out of inner being and not through imitation. Only gradually did those northern peoples, too, come to be fully imbued by imitative art.

From imitative to true artistic creation in our time

Nowadays, however, we are living in an age when human beings must again find their way into the spiritual world if there is to be a renewal of art. There must be a transition from imitation to a true artistic creation. The imitative arts reached their prime in the creations of Raphael and Michelangelo. Now, however, we face a different challenge. We have to enter consciously into the spiritual world and bring down the forms and colours living in the spiritual sea of the cosmos flowing all around us. A beginning must be made. Something must be brought down from the spiritual world that cannot be achieved by imitating what our senses perceive all around us. I have already spoken about the extent to which this conception is flowing into the forms of our building, and on another occasion we will consider this new conception of art in painting. Today my endeavour was to deepen the feelings and perceptions which must be ours if we are really to understand the transformation that must come about before the old forms of art can pass over into new ones.

I hope that especially those friends whose unselfish and devoted labours are revealed each day, as they struggle for the forms needed by our building, will work hard at this; so that, even if only in a primitive way as yet, they may achieve the beginning of a spiritualized art. I hope that they will find more and more enthusiasm and ever greater joy in the awareness that the world spirit calls on us to help in the task of establishing in human evolution those things that must be established in our own fifth post-Atlantean epoch and in the transition to the sixth epoch. By understanding this we join forces with the world spirit at work in human evolution, of which we try to gain knowledge through true and truly experienced spiritual science. All the impulses of this spiritual science can pass over into artistic feeling, artistic activity and experience of the cosmos. Genuine enthusiasm and devotion are necessary, and they will grow within us if we lovingly rise to the spirit which has guided mankind from the cosmic beginning of evolution, which will not forsake us if we dedicate ourselves to it with upright hearts and if our labours are not a sentimental prayer, but one arising from the power flowing into our inner being from the world spirit.

This spirit will lead us if we are filled with the inspiration of the knowledge that the work of our hands and souls can be guided by the power of the spirit in them.

May awareness of these things continue to inform our work.

THE CREATIVE WORLD OF COLOUR
The challenge for the artist is to express through the soul all that lives in his idea of the world

Lecture Five, Dornach, 26 July 1914

The need for a holistic art in our age of specialization

Today we will continue our study of various aspects of art. These lectures are intended to help us in regard to the thoughts which should imbue the work we are engaged in. If we want to find the right thoughts with which to accompany the task we are just beginning to tackle, it may be helpful to contemplate human achievements in art and their connection with civilization.

Herman Grimm, an intuitive student of art in the nineteenth century, made a rather startling statement about Goethe. He said that the world would not really appreciate the most important aspect of Goethe's work until around the year 2000.[1] Looking around us now this does not seem particularly surprising. To Herman Grimm, Goethe's greatest significance does not lie in the fact that he was a poet who created any particular single work of art, but that his creativity drew on the fullness of his human nature; every detail of his creative activity came from the fullness of the human being. Our age is indeed still very far from comprehending this fullness of humanity represented in an individual such as Goethe.

Although specialization in science is frequently criticized, this is not my reason for mentioning Grimm's thoughts about Goethe, for it is often necessary to specialize in science. More far-reaching than specialization in science is the way everything in modern life is getting specialized. As a result of this each individual soul, constricted within some particular sphere of specialized conceptions or ideas, grows less and less capable of understanding other souls who specialize in a different sphere. In a sense all human beings have become 'specialists' as far as their souls are concerned. This strikes us forcefully when we examine the way art has been evolving. It shows how necessary it is for there to be a new, comprehensive understanding, however primitive initially, of culture as a whole, in all its aspects. A new, overall view of culture and spiritual life will lead to forms of art that are artistic.

There is no need to embark on a very extensive study in order to prove the truth of this, so let us draw on something near at hand, quite a small point in the numerous irrelevant and often ridiculous attacks that are made against our spiritual movement nowadays.

Attacks on the anthroposophists' use of art in architecture

People feel quite justified in trying to slander us in the eyes of the world. They fabricate offences out of thin air. We are accused of having created buildings shaped in a way that seems to us appropriate for our work. We are reproached for having coloured walls in some of our meeting rooms. Our Goetheanum is thought eccentric and quite unnecessary for what is termed 'genuine theosophy'. This 'genuine theosophy' is thought to be a kind of psychic hotch-potch, teeming with obscure sensations and glorying in the fact that the soul can unfold a higher ego which has, however, purely egoistic intentions. From the point of view of this obscure psychic hotch-potch, people think that it is superfluous for a spiritual content to be expressed in outer form—and indeed it must be admitted that our attempts at outer form are only a primitive beginning. Such people think it is acceptable to chatter away about obscure sensations and divine egos wherever they happen to be; they cannot understand why it might be necessary to use 'eccentric' forms to give expression to something.

We cannot expect to find any capacity for real thought in people who fabricate this kind of reproach—in fact, we can expect such capacity from very few people at the present time. However, it is essential that we ourselves reach clarity on these points. Without such clarity we will not find the right answers to questions that arise in our soul.

Art needs to arise from the artist's soul in tune with his time

Let me draw your attention to Carstens, an artist of decided talent who made his mark at the end of the eighteenth century as a

The First Goetheanum from the north-east

draftsman and painter.[2] I do not propose to evaluate his art or describe his work, nor shall I tell you the story of his life. However, I do want to point out that he certainly possessed great talent for drawing, if not for painting. In the soul of Carstens we find his artistic longing, but we can also see what was lacking in him. He wanted to draw his ideas, to embody them in painting, but he was not in the position of men like Raphael or Leonardo,[3] or Dante— to take an example from poetry. Raphael, Leonardo and Dante were all imbued with a culture that teemed with sense and meaning, a culture that filled and surrounded the souls of human beings. There was a profound reason why Raphael painted madonnas. The essence of the madonna lived in human hearts and souls, and in the very highest sense something streamed from the soul of the public and flowed towards the creations of these great artists. When Dante set out to transport the human soul into spiritual realms he merely had to draw his material from something that was resounding in every soul. These artists possessed in their own souls the substance of the culture of their respective time.

In any work belonging to the culture of its own time, however obscure, we shall find connecting links with an element that was living in all human souls, right down to the humblest circles. The scholars in the cultural environment out of which Raphael created his madonnas were themselves thoroughly imbued with the idea of the madonna. In this sense artistic creations appear as expressions of the general, homogeneous culture of their time.

It was this that appeared again uniquely in Goethe in a manner only possible at the turn of the eighteenth to the nineteenth century. It is because this is so little understood in our times that, in Herman Grimm's opinion, we shall have to wait until the year 2000 before an understanding for it will become generally possible again.

Carstens, for example, turned to Homer's *Iliad* and what he read there he impressed into the forms he drew. The attitude of the eighteenth and early nineteenth century towards Homer's characters is so immensely different from that of Raphael's soul towards the madonna figures or indeed towards any other motif of his time. In the epochs of great art, the content of art is immediately perceptible because it flows from something that moves the innermost being of man. But in the nineteenth century a period began when artists had to make an effort to find the content of their creations. Very quickly the artist became a kind of 'cultural hermit' who was only concerned with himself and of whom people had to ask: 'What is this artist's own personal relationship with the figures he creates?' In this respect, a study of the history of painting in the nineteenth century would reveal the true state of affairs.

Modern coldness and indifference to art

Thus there gradually arose not only the indifference to art but the coldness towards it that exists nowadays. Think of someone in a modern city walking through a picture gallery or an exhibition of paintings. His soul is not moved by what he sees for it is something unfamiliar to him. He is faced, in a sense, by a multitude of riddles which he can only solve when he has reached an understanding of how the particular artist relates to his subject. The onlooker's soul is faced with purely individual riddles, and the significant thing is that although people imagine they are solving riddles to do with art, they are, in the vast majority of cases, not grappling with art riddles at all but merely with psychological ones to do with the way a particular artist sees nature or views the world. But such questions are of no importance when we examine the ages of great art. There both artist and onlooker face real tasks, aesthetic tasks, for there the manner in which the painting is to be done is what really concerns the painter, whereas the content, the substance of the painting is merely something that anyway flows around him and with which he is thoroughly imbued. You could say that today's painters are observers rather than artists; they observe the world from their particular point of view and what they happen to notice, because of their particular temperament, they paint. They tackle psychological themes, problems of philosophy or history, while the essential artistic question of how the painting is to be approached is something that has become almost entirely irrelevant in our time. People no longer have the capacity, or indeed the heart, to perceive art in its essence, which is to perceive the manner, rather than simply the content.

Art cannot arise from abstractions

Our present conception of the world—theoretical through and through—must bear a good part of the blame for this. Practical as people have become in technical, industrial and commercial affairs, they have grown eminently theoretical in the way they think about the world. Building a bridge between modern science and the artist's view of the world is not only fraught with difficulty, but few people have any desire to do so anyway. Goethe's statement that art is a manifestation of hidden laws of nature that would otherwise never be expressed is entirely incomprehensible for our time, though a few people may imagine they understand it.[4] Our age holds fast to the most external and abstract natural laws that are based on even more abstract mathematical foundations; it will not countenance any deeper understanding of reality that goes beyond a purely mathematical way of looking at things. It is therefore no wonder that our age has lost the living element of soul which can sense what is really at work in the cosmos as a whole and what must flow to us from the cosmos and all its workings if art is to come into being.

Art will never emerge from scientific concepts, let alone from abstract anthroposophical conceptions! At best these will generate insipid allegories or rigid symbols, but certainly nothing artistic. Thought and imagination about the world is today inherently inartistic; it even seeks to be inartistic.

The animal and colour

Take colours; what have they become for modern science? Waves in the ether, the most abstract part of matter, waves measured in frequencies. Try to imagine how far removed these waves in the ether are from the living essence of colours. How can people help entirely forgetting to pay proper attention to the dynamic and reality of colours? At the end of the previous lecture I mentioned how the element of colour lives and flows all around us; how with our soul we live within this flowing element.

I also pointed out that a time will come when people will once again see the living connection between the world of flowing colours and the way creatures and objects in the external world are coloured.

This is difficult today because during earth evolution human beings have to develop their ego and for this reason they have risen out of the flowing sea of colour so that they now see the world purely with their ego. Human beings have risen up out of the sea of colour, whereas animals still live submerged within it. The fact that creatures have feathers or fur of green, brown, red, black or white is connected with the way each animal soul is related to the sea of flowing colour. As we perceive external objects with our ego, an animal perceives them with its astral body; into the astral body flow the forces living in the group-soul of the animal.[5] It is nonsense to imagine that animals, even higher animals, see the world as human beings see it. At present there is no understanding of these things. People imagine that a horse sees them in the same way as they see it. Since the horse has eyes, what is more natural than to imagine that it sees us just as we see it. Yet this is complete nonsense. Without some degree of clairvoyance, a horse would no more see a human being than a human being without clairvoyance would see an angel, for human beings simply do not exist for the horse as physical beings, but only as spiritual beings. It is only because the horse has a degree of clairvoyance that it can perceive human beings standing above it rather like angels. What horses see in us is quite different from what we see in them. Even for higher animals we are like ghosts. If animals could speak—not in the way they are sometimes made to 'speak' nowadays, but in their own language—we would soon see that it would never occur to them to see us as resembling themselves, for they see us as higher, ghostly beings. We may see human beings as creatures of flesh and blood, but animals certainly do not. To the modern mind this of course sounds utterly nonsensical, which only goes to show how far our present age is removed from the truth.

Because of the way their astral body and group-soul are related, animals are receptive to the living creativity of colour. Just as we see an object that arouses our desire, and then stretch out to grasp it with our hands, so does an impression made in the whole animal organism, by the direct creative power in the colour, create a desire that flows into feathers or fur, colouring the animal. As I mentioned in the previous lecture, people today cannot even understand why the polar bear is white. Its white colour is the effect produced by its environment; and when the polar bear 'whitens' itself, this is, at a different level and in terms of desire, the same as when a person, seeing a rose, reaches out to pick it. The effect of the environment on the polar bear is to release a desire that makes it cover itself in whiteness.

The human being and colour

For us this living within the very essence of colour has passed into the substrata of our being because we would never have been able to develop our ego had we remained so wholly immersed within colour that our response, say, to the rosy hue of dawn would have been the desire to impress these tints, through creative imagination, into certain parts of our skin, as was still the case during the ancient Moon period.[6] In that time, observing a natural drama, such as the dawn, resulted in the colour being reflected back into the human being's own colouring; it suffused a person's whole being and was then outwardly expressed in parts of that person's body. This living within the flowing sea of colour, even with the physical body, had to cease during the Earth period so that in our ego we could develop our own view of the world. In our outer form we had to become neutral with regard to the sea of colour. The colour of our skin, as it has developed in the temperate climates of the earth, is essentially an expression of the ego, an expression of absolute neutrality in the face of external waves of colour; it is a consequence of man's emergence from the flowing sea of colour. Let us not forget, however, that the most elementary fact gleaned from spiritual science is that it is the human being's task to find the way back again.

Physical body, ether body and astral body were developed respectively during the ancient Saturn, Sun and Moon ages, and in the current age of Earth the ego is coming into being. As explained in my book *Theosophy*,[7] human beings must find ways and means to make their astral body spiritual once more, so that it can be filled with what the ego has won. In spiritualizing the astral body and so discovering the way back, human beings must find again the flowing, surging waves of colour out of which they emerged so that their ego might develop. This development was just like rising up out of the sea and looking around at what is above the waves rather than within or beneath them.

The painter needs to live into the world of colour

If we are not entirely to lose the capacity to live in and with the world, the time has come for us to begin our immersion in the spiritual powers that lie behind the physical realm. We must find ways of not merely looking at colours, and painting them on to surfaces, but of really living with them and experiencing their innate living qualities. This cannot be done, for instance, by merely gawping at the way different colours react with one another in painting. The only way to do it is once again to submerge our soul into the elemental forces of colour, that is into the way red flows, or blue flows, when the colours come alive for us. This can only be done by bringing alive the essence of colour in such a way that instead of arriving at colour symbolism—which would, of course, be the greatest mistake—we really discover the quality that is innate in colour, innate in the same way as the quality of laughter is innate in someone who is laughing. But since we have emerged with our ego from the flowing world of colour we can only do this by finding our way back into that world. If we can do no more than see some red here and some blue there [*drawing on the blackboard*] then we shall never manage to reach a living experience of what colour really is; and we shall be even less successful if we make intellectual interpretations of colour by seeing red as a symbol of one thing and blue of another. We must learn to surrender our whole soul to what speaks to us out of the colour. Then, when confronted with red, we shall feel an aggress-ive element coming towards us, something that wants to attack us. If women were to go about dressed all in red, a person possessed of a delicate sense for colour could gain the impression, simply from the colour of their dresses, that they were all about to attack him. In red there is a quality of aggression; it comes towards us. Blue, on the other hand, recedes; it goes away from us, leaving us with a wistful sense of longing.

The dynamics of red and blue

The distance modern people have travelled from any such understanding of colour is illustrated by what I have already said about Hildebrand, an excellent artist, who maintains that colour on a surface is simply that and nothing more; a surface is overlaid with colour—that is all—whereas a form can represent distance. Yet colour actually expresses much more than distance, and the fact that even an artist of Hildebrand's calibre cannot sense this, is a revealing symptom of the way colour is regarded nowadays. You cannot gain a living sense of the way colour is alive if you are unable to make the transition from rest to movement, thus rea-lizing that a red disc comes towards you while a blue one recedes; they move in opposite directions. [See Plate 1a.][8]

Immersing ourselves in this living essence of colour we then take further steps. As we begin to believe what the colours are telling us we realize that we can no longer imagine two discs like these standing still. To do so we would have to deaden all our sensitivity, for our feeling immediately tells us that the red and blue discs are revolving around one another, the one coming towards the observer while the other recedes. The red part of a figure reacts with the blue part in such a way that the colours bring it to life; because its colours shine the figure enters into the living world.

Colour gives soul to a form

Forms, on the other hand, are at rest, stationary. But the moment a form is given colour, the inner movement of the colour lifts the form out of its resting condition, so that the liveliness of the world and of the spirit flows through the form. As soon as you colour a form you endow it with cosmic soul because the colour does not belong exclusively to the form; it forces the form to relate to its environment, indeed to the whole universe. Colouring a form feels like going towards it and endowing it with soul qualities. You breathe soul into the dead form when you bring it alive with colour.

We need only draw a little nearer to this living, inner weaving of colours and we shall feel as though we are not confronting them on a level but standing either a little above or a little below them; we also feel how the colour comes alive. Someone who thinks in abstractions and merely gawps at the colours without bringing them to life inwardly, will see a red sphere revolving around a blue one, but he will not feel the need to vary the movement in any way. He may be a genius in mathematics or metaphysics, but he does not know how to live with colour as long as he sees it plodding like a dead thing from one place to the next. This is not what happens if you really live with colour, for then it radiates and changes all the time. Red, for example, strides along, driving before it a kind of aura of orange, of yellow and of green. [*Drawing begins again.*] And blue, when it moves, will drive something else on before it, which I would draw if I had the proper chalks. [See Plate 1a.]

What you have is a play of colours. Something takes place when you share the experiences of the colours, so that red seems to be on the attack, while blue recedes; you feel like running away from red, or warding it off, whereas you want to pursue blue with longing. If you could experience the living essence in the movement of red and blue, drawn so very inadequately here on the blackboard, you would inwardly accompany the living and moving surge of the colour; your soul would be in sympathy with the whirl of attacks and longings, flight and prayerful surrender, flowing there before your eyes.

If you were then to add this in an artistic way to a form which in itself is in repose, you would wrest it from this state of repose. The moment we have a form to which we add colour, instead of the form in repose we have living movement that does not belong to the form alone but also to the forces weaving around it. By filling it with soul you wrest the merely material aspect of the form from its repose.

The origins of our experience of red and blue

Surely something like this must have been 'painted into' this world by the creative elemental powers of the universe. Everything, indeed, which human beings are to receive through powers of longing is something that can find expression in blue. We must bear this as a forming, shaping principle in our head, while all that finds expression in the red must be borne within us in a form that flows upward into our brain from the rest of our physical body. These two currents are active in the building of our brain. Around us is the world for which we long. This is perpetually being flooded by what surges up from our own body. By day, in the physical body, what the blue half contains flows more intensely than what is contained in the red and yellow half; and by night the opposite is the case. What is generally termed the two-petalled lotus flower is a true image of what I have portrayed here; it reveals to the seer precisely such colours and movements. Nobody will really be able to fathom what shapes the upper part of the human head, if he cannot follow this flow of colour that is hidden within the human being.

A living art will be discovered through the elemental world

Art must endeavour to plunge once more into the life of the elements. It has observed and studied nature long enough; it has tried for long enough to solve all kinds of riddles of nature and depict in another form all that can be observed by penetrating into nature. The life of the elements is, however, dead so far as modern art is concerned. Air, water, light—all are dead in the way they are painted nowadays. Form presented to us in modern sculpture is dead. A new art will be born when human souls learn to penetrate to the depths of the elemental world, for this world is alive. People may argue against this; they may think that it ought not to be, but such argument is only the outcome of their inertia. Either we enter with our whole being into the world of the elements, absorbing into ourselves the spirit and soul of the external world and expressing it in art, or we allow art increasingly to become the work of the human soul in isolation. This could, of course, reveal many interesting things about the psychology of certain souls, but it will never lead to what art alone can achieve. These things belong to the far distant future, but we must go forward to meet this future with eyes that have been opened by spiritual science. To do otherwise is to look only into the dead and dying aspects of mankind's future.

This is why we must seek for inner connection between all our forms and colours and the spiritual knowledge that moves the inmost depths of our soul. We must seek for what lives in the spirit in the same way as the madonnas lived in Raphael, enabling him to become the painter of madonnas. The madonnas were living in Raphael's very being just as they were living in the learned men, the peasants in the fields and the craftsmen of his time. That is why he became the true painter of madonnas. Only when we succeed in bringing into our forms in a purely artistic sense, without symbolism or allegory, all that lives in our idea of the world—not as abstract thought, dead knowledge or science but as living substance of the soul—only then will we divine something of what is meant by the artistic development indicated here.

A true work of art cannot be a symbol—it is itself

Thus there must be unity between what is created externally and all that permeates the soul in its inmost depths—a unity like that found in Goethe as the result of a special karma. Bridges must be built between what are still for many people no more than abstract conceptions in spiritual science and what flows from hand, chisel and paint brush. This bridge-building is hindered today by a culture that is in many respects superficial and abstract and will not allow thoughts to come alive. This explains the appearance of the wholly groundless idea that spiritual knowledge might bring about the death of art. In some ways it has done this very thing because of all the allegorizing and symbolizing that goes on, the perpetual questioning as to what this means and what that signifies. I have repeatedly pointed out that people should not keep on asking what things mean or signify, just as we do not ask what the larynx signifies. The larynx does not 'signify' anything; it is a living organ for human speech. In the same way we must regard all that lives in the forms and the colours here in our building as a living organ of the spiritual world. We shall fail to achieve true spiritual knowledge so long as we persist in hunting for symbols and allegories and go on asking what things mean. We shall not succeed so long as we interpret myths and legends as allegories and symbols instead of sensing the living breath of the spirit that weaves throughout the universe, recognizing how this spirit enters into the characters of myths and fairy tales.

The Goetheanum as a beginning

A beginning must, however, be made, imperfect though it will be. No one should imagine that we take this beginning to be the perfect thing; but like many other objections to our spiritual movement made today, it is nonsense to say that our building is not an essential part of this spiritual movement. We are already aware of the facts which people take it upon themselves to point out. We know perfectly well that all the foolish chatter about the 'higher self', all the rhapsodies in regard to the 'divinity of the soul', can equally well be expressed inside buildings that conform with present-day standards. We are also well aware that the concepts and ideas of spiritual science can be studied in premises of every kind. But over and above this we know that if a living spiritual science is to be poured into souls it will need an environment that is different from any that the dying culture of our day may produce.

The ideals of our spiritual science that must pour into our soul should be taken more and more seriously, but we have a long way to go before this seriousness, this inner driving force of the soul will have become part of our very being. It is all too easy to speak

The First Goetheanum—detail of ceiling painting by Rudolf Steiner above the stage: a variety of beings appearing out of a sea of colour

about spiritual science and its expression in the outer world in a way that totally misses its essence. Thus the virulent attacks that seem to be raining down on us at the moment first describe all manner of fantastic nonsense that has not the remotest connection with us, and then they proceed to attack that nonsense.[9] The world is so little capable of accepting a new spirituality that it has to invent a wholly grotesque caricature against which it then proceeds to rail. Some people think we ought to dispute all this. We can certainly raise objections, but you cannot really dispute something that bears no resemblance to what is actually the case. To be taken very much to heart, however, is the sense for the truth that lies at the foundation of all these things. With a genuine sense for truth we can become strong in all that spiritual science will bring to us and reveal externally in the material world. We can become strong even though the world today has neither tolerance nor understanding for what spiritual science represents.

Experiencing colour

We can celebrate the inner confluence of our soul with spiritual science in no better way, perhaps, than by immersing ourselves in questions such as that of colour. In experiencing the living flow of colour we transcend the measure of our own stature and live in cosmic life. Colour is the soul of nature and the soul of the whole cosmos. We participate in this soul when we experience colour.

This was what I wanted to indicate today, in order next time to penetrate still more deeply into the nature of the world of colour and the essence of painting.[10]

I could not help interspersing my talk today with references to the attacks that are being made upon us from all sides, attacks emanating from a world incapable of understanding the aims of our anthroposophical movement. We can only hope that by a deepening of their being, those within our movement will be able to understand something truly symptomatic of our times: the falsehood and untruth that is creeping into people's conception of what is striving to find its place within today's culture. We most certainly have no wish to seclude our spiritual stream and shut it off from the world. The world can have as much as it is willing to receive, but one thing it will have to accept, if it is to understand us, and that is the unity of the whole human being, the unity which makes every separate human achievement the outcome of this full and complete being.

A beginning that will be taken further at the end of the twentieth century

In saying these things I do not mean to attack the present age. I speak with a feeling of sorrow because we can observe that the more our will and our efforts expand within this movement of ours, the more malicious—perhaps not consciously, but more or less unconsciously—do the opposing forces become. I have also said these things because the way in which such matters should be looked at is not yet fully understood even amongst ourselves. The unshakable standpoint must be that something new, a new beginning, is at least intended in our movement. What goes beyond this intention has, of course, yet to come. Our building can be no more than something we intend to take further, and those capable of taking our intention further will surely come—though perhaps not until that time of which Herman Grimm spoke, when he anticipated a complete understanding of Goethe being one day achieved. In order to understand Grimm's statement we need humility, but this is something signally lacking in present-day culture. Spiritual science, however, is well suited to bring within reach of our soul not only this humility but also a realization of the gravity of these things.

Now that the world can actually see something arising from our spiritual movement it is reacting in a way that may be depressing for us. So long as the movement was there merely in a spiritual sense, there was nothing to see. But now that the world is beginning to see something it cannot understand, dissonant trumpetings are to be heard from every quarter, and they are likely to increase. When we realize this we shall at first naturally feel sad, but an inner strength will make us able to take a stand on behalf of something that is to us not merely conviction, but life itself. Living, etheric strength will fill human souls; it will be something greater than theoretical convictions of which people are still so proud today. An earnest mood of soul will bring in its train the sure confidence that the foundations of our world and of our existence as human beings will be able to sustain us if we seek for them in the spiritual world. Sometimes we need this confidence more, sometimes less. Out of the sorrow caused by the echo which our spiritual movement is finding in the world, must grow the mood of strength about which I have spoken. This mood of strength derives from the knowledge that human life is rooted in the spirit and that the spirit will lead human beings out beyond the disharmony that now causes such sorrow. Out of the mood of strength will flow the energy we need.

Spiritual science has the potential to win through in the end

Today we have had to speak with sorrow about spiritual matters because there is such discrepancy between what we intend with our spiritual movement and the echo that is coming to meet it from the world at large. However, the disharmonies of the world will follow a different course once people have come to understand what the light of spiritual science can kindle in their hearts. Meanwhile, compared with our sorrow for the destiny of Europe just now, our sorrow for the troubles of our movement is but slight.[11]

As I speak these words to you I tremble with sorrow, yet at the same time I am filled with the living certainty that, whatever pain may be lying in wait for the people of Europe in the near or more distant future, we may be confident that the spirit will lead human beings through every wilderness to victory in the end. In these days of sorrow, in hours fraught with such gravity, we may in very truth, indeed we must, speak about spiritual science as something holy. For we may surely believe that however dimly the sun of spiritual science is shining today its radiance will increase until it is a sun of peace, of love and of harmony amongst all mankind.

Now that a time of darkness is looking in through our windows from the world at large, words of such gravity show that we are right to lavish all we have in heart and soul upon the seemingly narrower concerns of spiritual science.

APPENDIX

THE EVOLUTION OF ARCHITECTURE AT THE TURN OF EACH NEW MILLENNIUM
(Two fragments in note form)

I   The assault on humanity at each millennium[1]

Stuttgart, 7 March 1914

As the year AD 1000 approached, people in Europe lived in great fear of the end of the world which was anticipated as the physical dissolution of the earth in smoke and fog. Ahrimanic spirits had led people to believe that something dreadful was going to happen in the physical world, whereas in reality a great deal was happening in the spiritual world. At the turn of every millennium the spirits of Lucifer and Ahriman possess exceptional powers.

Human beings have no cause to be particularly proud of the decimal system, which is the predominant system of calculation today. Every such system is introduced to the world by certain spirits, and each system tends to clarify some facts and realities while obscuring others. In the decimal system it is Ahriman who exerts considerable influence. This system highlights the fact that at every millennium, around the year 1000, 2000 and so on, a particularly vigorous combined assault by Lucifer and Ahriman takes place, while during the other centuries they hold one another more in balance. During the ninth century of a millennium—and thus also in our ninth century of the second millennium—as a new millennium approaches, they join forces and together exert their influence on mankind. This fact underlies the popular belief that Lucifer and Ahriman are bound in chains for a thousand years and then released for a short period of time.

The influence of good powers at the millennium

At pre-Christian turns of the millennia—1000, 2000, 3000 BC—a particularly strong influence was also exerted simultaneously by good, progressive powers, so that the joint activity of Lucifer and

Ahriman was held in check, with exceptionally good results. Thus around the year 3000 BC the pyramids were built; around 2000 BC was the age of Abraham and all that resulted from it, as well as being the culmination of Babylonian culture; and around 1000 BC was the age of David in which the construction of Solomon's Temple was planned. In the year Nought, Christ appeared. We have often discussed how according to the Gospels, and especially the 'Fifth Gospel', Christ had to engage in combat with both Lucifer and Ahriman. Since the coming of Christ, however, the good, progressive spirits have no longer been able to intervene so effectively. Human beings have been exposed to the attacks of Lucifer and Ahriman, who have succeeded in confusing people's minds and making them fall prey to misconceptions of the approaching physical end of the world. It is always in the interest of Lucifer and Ahriman to relate events much too closely to the factors of space and time.

Around AD 1000 came the first proofs for the existence of God as presented by the Bishop of Canterbury, as well as the ideas introduced by his opponent, Roscelin. This was also the age when the popes, trampling on the principle of Christian humility, raised themselves up in external power, when the Emperor Henry IV was forced to humiliate himself in the presence of the Pope at Canossa, and when the entire established church adopted practices which aroused the derision of all the spirits of Ahriman.

These same ahrimanic spirits are now again making their influence felt as we approach the year AD 2000. But evolution swings like a pendulum. In AD 1000 the end of the world was anticipated, in AD 2000 exactly the opposite is expected, and in AD 3000 the end of the world will be anticipated once more; indeed, by then things will have come to such a pass that whole nations will be longing for the end. Without sentimentality it can be stated that dreadful times are approaching for the peoples of Europe.

Architecture at the millennium

Let us take architecture as an example and look at the influence exerted upon it. Around 3000 BC the pyramids were built. Around 2000 BC came the hut structures of the Age of Abraham, and around the year 1000 BC preparations were made for the Temple of Solomon. The new architectural impulse that was to have arisen around the year AD 1000 was suppressed by opposition from Lucifer and Ahriman. We see how the Norsemen (also known as Normans), who spread across western and central Europe from Scandinavia, attempted to express something in their timber constructions which they were unable to develop fully. Certain directions are intimated, but ahrimanic influence prevented their elaboration. Instead the Moorish culture evolved, coming from Cordoba and Granada, introducing the horseshoe arch and the pointed arch which supplanted the truly Christian rounded arch of Romanesque architecture. Anti-Christian influence is directly visible in Moorish architecture with its arches that run up into a point instead of being round. This is the mark of Ahriman. In architecture Ahriman worked as the Antichrist when he replaced rounded Romanesque arches with horseshoe and pointed arches. He worked thus through the Moors and also through the Turks, while preventing the appropriate development of architecture by the Norsemen whose wooden buildings were erected all over Europe but were unable to give to mankind what was intended. This is the reason why there are no great works of architecture from around AD 1000 such as we can find at earlier millennia.

The new architecture for AD 2000

Now the time has come to create a new architecture for the new millennium. The curved lines which Ahriman suppressed in Norse architecture must now find new expression, while other aspects are left out. The result will be our Dornach building, which will be the true successor to Norse timber architecture.

The people of Europe, however, are moving towards terrible times. We know that after the first third of this century Christ will be seen in his etheric form and that this will have a tremendous impact alongside all the tendencies of decline in this century. In former times, for example in AD 1000, people had to believe what Lucifer and Ahriman wanted to make them believe because they did not yet carry the true, conscious impulse of Christ within themselves. We, however, are no longer under any such constraint.

It is up to us freely to receive the new Christ-impulse, in order to resist Lucifer and Ahriman. In the twentieth century Lucifer and Ahriman will seize control especially over the name of Christ. People who no longer bear any trace of true Christianity will set themselves up as Christians. They will rage against those who not only observe what Christ said according to the Gospels but who also believe in the words: 'I am with you always until the end of all time on earth.' People who are guided by Christ's living, continuing impulse, will be derided. As AD 2000 approaches confusion and destruction will prevail. By then no splinter of our building in Dornach will be intact. When we look down from the spiritual world we will see everything destroyed and devastated. But by the year 2086 buildings will be arising throughout Europe which are dedicated to spiritual aims and which will resemble our Dornach building with its two cupolas. That will be the golden age for buildings in which spiritual life will flourish.

West front of Second Goetheanum, opened in 1928

II Facing up to public criticism[2]

Munich, 30 March 1914
(Introduction to a lecture)

Permit me to begin with a few words on a subject that may interest a number of our friends. Placing our building into the world is something we are bound by our karma to do. The criticism which our undertaking encountered as soon as the plan to erect a building here in Munich was conceived indicates that in this connection we have no choice but to disregard everything that is at variance with the convictions of spiritual science. We must accept as a matter of course that all outsiders will misconstrue our project. Because this undertaking of ours, which is so alien to the modern way of looking at things, will attract the attention of a wider public to our spiritual science, this will now become the butt of greater hostility than would otherwise have been the case. People cannot help noticing something that is placed right in front of their eyes, and thus more will become known about our spiritual science than we might have wished. The building will attract criticisms that will include spiritual science in their sweep, and the nature of these criticisms is there for all to see. We in turn must not flinch from the realization that what we are grappling with is the very heartbeat of the age in which we live.

The first millennium as a challenge to human evolution

At the approach of the year AD 1000, European souls far and wide sensed that something significant must be going on in evolution; and because perception had assumed increasingly materialistic forms they thought of this in terms of the physical end of the world. However, this was merely a materialistic interpretation of a universal law.

It is certainly true that events take place at the end of each millennium that are of consequence for the whole of human life. We have already pointed this out in connection with the approaching appearance of Christ's ether body which will become increasingly perceptible as the year AD 2000 draws near.

Significant spiritual events are always bound up in human evolution when these special periods approach. Although we are only at the beginning of our twentieth century, clairvoyant vision can see how luciferic and ahrimanic forces will increasingly encircle human beings as time goes on. Similarly, as AD 1000 was approaching, these luciferic and ahrimanic forces, working against the Christ-impulse in the world, spread misunderstanding in human souls about the end of the world.

If the same modes of thought prevailed today, people would again be speaking about the end of the world. At the time when the first Christian millennium was drawing to a close, anti-Christian impulses were asserting themselves not so much in tangible ideas as in the depths of soul development; these impulses introduced into the world thought-forms that are directly influenced by Ahriman and Lucifer.

Islam and the pointed arch

At that time an instrument of this influence was the Islamic culture of Arabia which spread across Africa to southern Europe. Rather than the actual dogmas of Islam and the ideas that were circulated throughout Spain, I mean the impulses that penetrated to the depths of people's souls. One such influence was exerted by a form of great significance: the arch that culminates in a point. This is one of Ahriman's marks, and such things are smuggled into human evolution.

The inspirers of Norse architecture and of the Goetheanum

When I was seeking the spirits who granted us the inspiration for the forms of our building at Dornach I discovered that these same spirits were the ones who had opposed Ahriman and Lucifer towards the close of the first millennium. When the Norse peoples migrated southwards from the north they brought with them architectural forms that were executed in wood. For the new architectural style we are inaugurating—although it will be imperfect because we have not the means with which to do better—we were inspired to create forms that emphasize roundness both on a large scale and in the smaller details. The difference is that the Norsemen left empty space where in our building we have forms filled with wood, and vice versa, what the Norsemen filled with wood is left empty, is free space, in our building.

It was necessary for us to obey the inspiring spirits more closely than they were obeyed at the end of the first millennium when they sought to oppose Lucifer and Ahriman.

Opposing powers and our will to work with Christ

Much has changed since then; many things have happened in the culture and spiritual life of human beings. In seeking to bring together all that we want to put into the forms of our building we must be quite clear that much of what is considered to be Christian and bears the name of Christ has, in fact, an anti-Christian effect, and that the most cunning device of luciferic and ahrimanic forces is to introduce anti-Christian impulses into the world in Christ's own name. We must become increasingly aware that, even in the individual forms, every single detail has to be accomplished in accordance with the progressive spiritual powers of humanity, even if the building can as yet only represent an imperfect beginning.

I did not intend to extol our building unduly with these words, but merely sought to imply something of which we must become aware. I wanted to inspire you all to love our building so that it will live in your hearts as something that must be willed, and not merely as a whim. The more we love our building the more shall we succeed in placing it before the world in a manner that accords with the wishes of the spirits working with the Christ-impulse in our present time.

Receive our building and all that is related to it into your hearts. Be aware that its inauguration at the end of this year will be an important event. It is our karma and not our fault that it is not being built here in Munich. Because of our destiny it is being executed in a solitary place, a place, however, whose situation makes it important for the life of the spirit in modern times.

THE REBUILDING OF THE GOETHEANUM
The design concept of the proposed new building at Dornach

I   Concerning the internal plans[3]

Dornach, 31 December 1923
(Extract from the morning lecture)

The plan will need to express the concrete construction

As you may imagine, I have recently given much thought to the design concept of the proposed new building here in Dornach, and the situation will most certainly necessitate the earliest possible execution of this design...

Today I want to begin by explaining the plan of the Goetheanum, and then tomorrow I shall speak more about the elevation, the façade. I want to shape the plan and the whole distribution of the space to be included in the Goetheanum in the following way.

The new Goetheanum will not be as round a building as the old one. You might well ask why I have not brought the model to show you, but you must not forget that this new Goetheanum is to be built of a relatively new material, *in situ* cast, steel-reinforced concrete. To give a concrete building a truly artistic character in keeping with this material is exceedingly difficult, and the solution poses considerable problems.

As you know, Dr Grosheintz has built a house close by which I sought to design in a style appropriate to concrete.[4] However, although I still believe that this style might be considered to some degree satisfactory for a dwelling—but only to some degree—I would not consider it right to build a second house to this same design. In any case it certainly has not yielded an architectural style for a Goetheanum built of concrete. For the new Goetheanum it will be necessary to depart from an essentially circular building and return to something more rectangular and less rounded—that is, a building with angles.

Eurythmeum from west, design 1923 by Rudolf Steiner

You can see what I intend to be a more angular style in the small building lower down the hill that is built to provide a hall for eurythmy practice.[5] Although it is not built in reinforced concrete, it shows that an angular building has considerable potential.

Extra floors will be provided

Since it is a question of providing a stage both for eurythmy and the Mystery Dramas, it will be necessary to combine an angular building with a circular one. In addition, the new Goetheanum will have to provide space for the various activities. We shall need art studios as well as a number of lecture rooms, since the single small White Hall, in which the fire broke out a year ago, turned out to be quite inadequate for our purposes. Hence the new Goetheanum will have to be built with a ground floor as well as an upper level.[6] The upper level will essentially comprise the large auditorium for audiences attending eurythmy performances, the Mystery Dramas, and other events. On the ground floor, directly beneath the auditorium, there will be smaller rooms, divided off by walls, which will provide space for artistic and scientific purposes.

I also intend to provide a room which will serve the administration of the General Anthroposophical Society, so that this can be carried out direct from the Goetheanum.

Two stages, one devoted to rehearsal

Out of the design concept I also want to solve a certain problem in what seems to me a practical way. The plan will be such that there will be a stage at the rear with a rounded form. (Please do not take any notice of the scale of this drawing.)

Blackboard sketch by Rudolf Steiner, 31 December 1923

The stage will essentially form a semi-circle. It will be enclosed by store-rooms. Extending forwards there will be at the upper level the auditorium and at the terrace level the various rooms, with a passage in between for general use. This will enable more freedom of movement in this new Goetheanum than there was in the old. In the old Goetheanum you stepped straight from a vestibule into the auditorium, direct from the outside. Here, so that there can be greater freedom of movement, there will be a heated area in which there will be ample opportunity to meet and converse, and which will give access to the various rooms on the terrace level.

Then, going up a staircase, you will come to a large auditorium from which you look on to the stage or the space where lectures and other events will take place.

The practical problem just referred to is this: in the old Goetheanum great inconvenience was caused by the fact that eurythmy rehearsals had to take place on the stage. When outside visitors

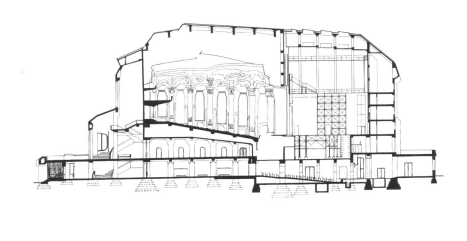

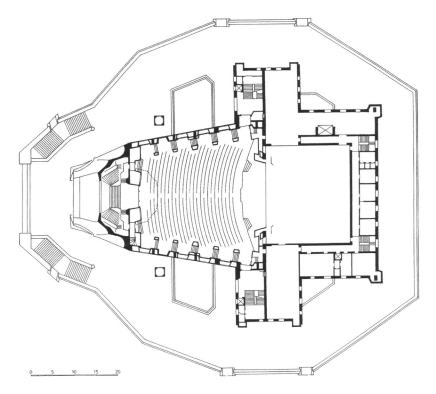

Second Goetheanum, plan and west/east section

came—and I hope they will continue to come in the future—they wanted to see everything; but the auditorium was needed for the work, so it was never possible to make a proper schedule for rehearsals and the preparation needed for performances.

I now want to solve this problem by having on the lower floor a stage of exactly the same size as the actual stage above. The upper one will serve for the actual performances while the one below, having identical measurements, will be for rehearsals only. So there will be a room down below which can serve for all rehearsals up to the dress rehearsal, thus leaving the upper auditorium free at all times. The area on the lower level will have an ante-room just for those taking part in rehearsals, where they may wait and sit down. On the upper level the stage will give straight on to the auditorium, which will be the same size on plan as the rectangular part of the building. In this way it will be possible to make practical use of all the available space.

The elevation of the new Goetheanum

It will not be necessary to make the new Goetheanum very much higher than the old Goetheanum, since I am not considering a new cupola. I am endeavouring to create a design for the roof which will consist of a series of flat surfaces arranged in relation to one another in a way that will, I believe, be no less aesthetically attractive than a cupola.

The new Goetheanum will be entered through a façade on the main west front which I shall describe tomorrow. There we shall find the staircase leading to the main auditorium; and below we shall have the passage-way from which the different rooms are reached, and so on. There will also be entrances at the sides. By making the stage space smaller on plan than the store area, and by extending the walls forwards, we will gain space for a variety of other rooms. At the top it will be possible to light the whole space with daylight, so that we can alternate between daylight, when it is there, and artificial light when we need it.

The importance of keeping abreast of the times

In this way we shall have a practical building in which space is used to the full. A great deal will be able to go on concurrently, compared to the old building where really only one thing at a time could take place.

You must bear in mind that this is not simply intended to be an improvement—a change which some might even consider a retrograde step. It is intended to take account of the whole development of our work. I have often stressed that if you want to live in reality and not in ideas, then the reality of time must be given particular recognition. Time is a reality, although it is difficult to recognize it as such. There are still people today who offer the same arguments for the threefold ordering of society as I was employing in 1919 with regard to the state of affairs which existed then. History is advancing so rapidly just now that statements made in 1919 already seem to be hundreds of years out of date. Thus, since things have after all been happening in the anthroposophical movement, you cannot build in 1924 as you did in 1913 or 1914. The design of the old Goetheanum arose in 1913/1914 simply out of the realization that an artistic space was required for the Mystery Dramas. At that time the space was really only intended for the Mystery Dramas and the lectures. So much has happened since those days, and I only wish that even more had been accomplished, but I hope that, even without the 75 million francs already mentioned, a great deal more will soon come to pass. This increase in activity must also be taken into consideration.

One thing that has happened since 1919 is that eurythmy has been developed.[7] In 1913 it did not yet exist, it has only developed since then. Therefore it cannot be maintained that what was good enough then is good enough now. Moreover, although I was assured at the time that the building could be executed at a cost of much less than one million German Marks, the cost in the end, as you know, was at least seven or eight times as much. So we do not want to do our sums in the abstract this time; we want to reckon with quite definite figures. The building must now be executed in such a way that we can begin to carry out what is contained in our Statutes as soon as possible. This can only happen if we build it in the manner described.

The artistic use of concrete

Even so, it will be possible to achieve forms with the intractable material of concrete that offer something new to the artistic eye.

The old forms of the Goetheanum—I shall have more to say to you about these things this evening[8]—will have to be consigned to history, which means to your hearts, my dear friends. Concrete forms will have to be entirely different. On the one hand much will have to be done to force the intractable material of concrete into forms which the soul's eye can follow artistically. On the other hand features that appear to be decorative will actually be the consequence of the concrete itself. You will see that with the help of artistic treatment, painting and sculpture, concrete can also be artistic.

Rudolf Steiner to have sole artistic charge of the new building

I ask you now to regard this idea as the seed out of which the new Goetheanum will actually emerge. I have asserted that I alone am to be allowed to work on the artistic creation of the Goetheanum. It will not be possible to take much account of even the best-intentioned advice or suggestions already offered. There is really no point in informing me about any other concrete buildings or telling me about factories that are working efficiently and so on. If

Second Goetheanum, model by Rudolf Steiner, March 1924

the Goetheanum is to be realized in concrete it will have to emerge from a single original design concept. Nothing that has so far been achieved in concrete can serve as a basis for what is to come into being here.

The auditorium of the Second Goetheanum looking south-east (above), and looking south (below), as completed 1998

II   Concerning the external appearance[9]

Dornach, 1 January 1924
(Extract from the morning lecture)

*Letting the same creative forces of the old building come to
expression in the new*

... I would now like to pass on to the question of the rebuilding of
the Goetheanum and add a few remarks to what I said yesterday.
You will recall that I attempted to approach the exterior design of
the First Goetheanum, as far as I was then able, as a construction
problem. The speed with which the building was expected to come
into being complicated many aspects unnecessarily. Nevertheless I
believe that an exterior design was found for the essentially
rounded building which portrayed on the outside, in portals,
windows, cornices and so on, the inner content of the Goetheanum.
   As I attempted to explain to you yesterday, the impression is to
be of a building that is partly circular and partly rectangular, having
no longer a ground plan that is circular. It will be necessary to find a
modern style that is appropriate for concrete as a building material.

The treatment of the openings: load-bearing elements

Something like this is always exceedingly difficult. It is of course
easier to work out the forms in the abstract first and then choose
the material than it is to accept the material as a given necessity
and model forms from it that are also partly determined by the
circumstances which I described to you yesterday. Since we do not
have time to go into more detail, I shall show you one essential
feature, the underlying theme of the portals and windows. From
this example you will see how I want to let the inner creative force
that was latent in the old forms assert itself anew in the forms
moulded from this intractable material, concrete.
   I would like the walls coming down from the roof, which is
shaped in flat surfaces, to give the eye a definite impression of load.
At the same time I want the design to show how this downward

pressure is caught and held by the portals and by the window surrounds. I also want to create the impression of a portal drawing you in, or a window drawing in the light, ushering it into the space within. Moreover, I want the overall form to reveal how the Goetheanum is to be a kind of shelter for those who seek the spirit within it; even the portal will have to express this. Here is a rough sketch of what it will look like [See Colour Plate 1b.]

The example of the new west front

For instance, on the west front the roof will rise up like this. So I want the next thing appearing after the roof to be a kind of small form growing out of this roofing. Let me make it easier for you to see by using different colours to draw what will, of course, be all the same colour. This will jut out [*lemon-yellow*]; it will be immediately above the head of someone who is standing before the portal, about to enter. Below that will be what could be taken for a portion of a pentagon [*orange*]. The remainder of the pentagon would be above. The whole of this is carried by a form which recedes [*blue*]. So what you remember as rounded forms in the earlier Goetheanum will here appear angular. You must imagine that *this* comes forward like a kind of roof [*lemon-yellow*], *this* recedes inwards [*blue*], and *this* becomes visible in the background [*white*]. The whole will be supported by a pillar shape to the left and to the right in such a way that this pillar receives the protective form which appears above the head of the one who enters; this protective form is received into another form [*golden-yellow*] like this, but at the same time it carries the roof part with an appropriate form that grows out of it.

This design will be used for both the side and main portals and for the windows. It will enable us to achieve a really integrated external experience, showing on the one hand how the load pressing down from above is carried and on the other hand how the pillars rise up in order to give adequate support to that which comes out from the inside, revealing itself and needing to be received.

Integrated organic whole

The essential thing about an angular building is the harmony

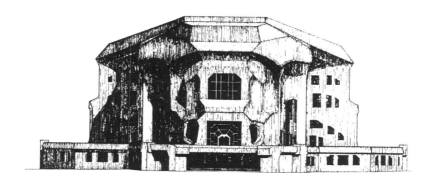

Second Goetheanum, west elevation and south elevation

between the forces of support and load. If we are to carry this out in a building that follows organic principles, every part must reveal the indwelling character of the totality. The pillars in the old building reached from bottom to top. Now they will be metamorphosed so that on the lower level they will develop like roots—architecturally conceived, of course. Out of these the actual pillars will grow on the upper level, becoming bearers of the whole. They will then bring the forms of the roof to completion from within outwards. The roof will not be terminated horizontally but rather in the way the cupola was terminated. The pillars will be metamorphosed into supporting elements while at the same time expressing what in the old Goetheanum was to have been expressed in the roundness of the building.

We shall have to take pains to calculate how basic the forms will have to be—merely hinted at, perhaps—in order to keep the whole building, given this design, within 3 to 3½ million francs. Once we have made this decision—and I do not believe that any other is possible—and assuming the willingness of our friends to make sacrifices, then we shall, I hope, be in a position to begin construction. The building will then rise as a new Goetheanum on the site of the old, albeit in a more basic and simple form.

Second Goetheanum, detail of north-west elevation

III The reconstruction of the Goetheanum

Basle, 25/26 October 1924
Article in *Die Basler Nachrichten*

An architecture in harmony with anthroposophy

Now that the Solothurn government has in principle approved the plans for the new Goetheanum, the Anthroposophical Society will soon be commencing construction. There is still a minimum of work to be done at the drawing board and by the accountants to incorporate alterations requested by Dornach parish council and by the government.

Being constructed in concrete instead of wood, the new building will look very different from the old Goetheanum. The artistic execution of the design will have to conform to the limitations imposed by this new material. Quite clearly, the Goetheanum cannot be erected in just any existing architectural style since it is to serve anthroposophy, which does not intend to function one-sidedly as a theoretical philosophy but is, in fact, an all-embracing model for human life as a whole, conducted in unison with the will of the spirit. It is the anthroposophical view of the spirit that must generate any artistic style it may display to the world. Not to build in its own style would be tantamount to denying its very essence. This is particularly true in a building that is intended to serve the needs of anthroposophy.

A style true to the construction material

An unprejudiced artistic appraisal of the new Goetheanum's style will find that although it does not reject any styles of the past that may still be relevant today, it is not influenced by them either. Instead it draws on the fundamental principles that lie at the heart of the feeling for style as such. However, the shapes and forms in which a style is expressed are to some extent governed by the material used. Because of the relative softness of wood in the old Goetheanum it was possible to shape every detail of the inner working space in accordance with the spirit of anthroposophical research. With concrete, on the other hand, it is necessary to search for forms that let the space which is to be enclosed determine them in such a way as to make the space suitable for anthroposophical work. Essentially, straight lines and flat surfaces have turned out to be suitable for exterior walls and the roof. The way these are angled in relation to one another will fit in with the overall plan for the building. Nearer to the openings and immediately surrounding them the lines and surfaces will be of a somewhat smaller scale and more varied in their arrangement.

The entire building is to be raised by placing it on a podium with a terrace which in its turn will be artistically shaped on all sides. The visitor will be able to walk round the whole building on this terrace that affords views of the beautiful surrounding countryside.

The building itself will comprise a lower floor containing studios, lecture and practice rooms, offices and so on, and an upper floor housing the auditorium for 900–1000 people. At the rear, the lower floor will have a rehearsal stage and the upper floor the stage for public performances. The exterior of the building will truly depict in an artistic way the experience of the spirit unfolding

Second Goetheanum from the west, on podium of First Goetheanum

within. Wide, sweeping steps will lead up from ground level to the entrances on the terrace. The exterior forms will have to evolve from the necessary arrangement of interior space on the two levels. The roof—no longer domed—with its arrangement of lines and flat surfaces will, at the front, have to follow the rise of the auditorium, and, at the back, the enclosing walls of the two stages with their storage rooms. In the interior the task will be to create a space which can serve as a lecture hall as well as a theatre for performances of eurythmy and the Mystery Dramas. For example the pillars will be shaped to depict the way the space extends upwards. Thus once again, as in the old Goetheanum, whatever anthroposophy has to convey may be sensed in the overall plan as well as in the detailed forms used to construct the building in which it intends to work.

The idea of the building has led to something monumental manifesting through the architectural conception. What has been striven for in the whole as well as all its details will not manifest in the architecture as something deceitful. On the contrary, it will appear as an artistic and completely honest reflection of that which is created within out of spirit knowledge. The creator of this design is of the opinion that in this way something has been achieved to which the taste of an unbiased general public may respond positively, even where there is no knowledge of anthroposophy or indeed any wish for such knowledge.

IV The Second Goetheanum

Basle, 1 November 1924
Article in *Die National-Zeitung*

The rebuilding of the Goetheanum has given rise to considerable discussion in the press and aroused interest in the widest circles. We are now in a position to publish a picture of the future building and we have also invited Dr Rudolf Steiner to expound on the concept of the building. (Editor)

The proposed rebuilding has posed no easy task for the manifestation of its architectural conception. A total reorientation was necessary since the old building was constructed essentially in wood while the new one is to be built entirely in concrete. In addition, the design had to be compatible with the essence of the anthroposophy which is to be cultivated within its walls. Anthroposophy draws on spiritual sources from which flow both the knowledge of the spirit and also, for those sensitive to it, the shapes and forms of artistic style. It seeks the primordial forces of knowledge which are also the very origins of artistic form and design. Thus it would be grotesque if its own building were to be designed by someone with quite different aesthetic sentiments and with only a superficial feeling for the essence of anthroposophy. This place of work can only be designed by someone for whom the experience of every detail comes from the same spiritual vision as does the knowledge contained in every word spoken out of anthroposophy.

Organic forms in the old wooden Goetheanum

Because of the softness of wood it was possible to shape space in a manner that conformed with the way nature shapes organic forms. An organism as a whole creates for even its smallest parts—an ear lobe, for example—a shape that cannot be other than it is. By entering artistically into the way nature creates organic forms and raising this through creative fantasy to a spiritual level it was possible to create an 'organic style of architecture' as opposed to

Second Goetheanum

one based merely on static or dynamic forces. Thus there was in the old Goetheanum a vestibule which visitors entered before going into the main auditorium. The forms carved in the wood indicated quite clearly that it was a space ready to receive people coming in from outside. Another factor that determined the way the wood was shaped was the need for everything to fit in organically with the building as a whole. From this, in turn, arose the exterior design, which revealed artistically how the building was both formed and articulated to meet the requirements of the anthroposophical work taking place within it.

The convex character of the new concrete building

The architectural conception now has to be handled quite differently since it is a question of using concrete rather than wood. For this reason it took nearly a year before the new design model could be made. With wood, the shape of the space is carved into the material; a form arises from a concave, hollowing-out treatment of the main surface. With concrete, on the other hand, the form is convex, a bulging-out of the main surface defining the boundary of the space required. This also shows in the way the exterior forms come about. Surfaces, lines and angles all have to be handled according to the way the forms and shapes on the inside press outwards into them, making themselves visible.

In addition to all this we shall have to work more economically with space in this second Goetheanum than was the case in the first. This basically consisted of a single space that was able to provide artistic surroundings for both lectures and performances. There will now be two levels, the lower one comprising offices, lecture rooms and a rehearsal stage, and the upper one the auditorium and main stage, which can also be used for lectures.

Architectural design responds to the practical necessities

The artistic shaping of the outside lines and surfaces had to evolve from this interior design. The way the roof is shaped is a case in point—it will not be domed this time. When penetrating the architectural forms with feeling it will be discovered how we have attempted to solve the task of finding an artistic solution that follows the rise of the auditorium at the front while at the rear it follows the enclosing walls of the stage with its storage rooms. Unbiased artistic appraisal may reveal how the underlying necessities in the design of the plan have been followed through in the whole concept of the architecture, including the daring execution of the western façade.

The building is to stand on a terrace which will enable people to walk round the building at a level higher than ground level. Wide, sweeping stairs will lead up from ground level to the entrances on the terrace. Cloakrooms and other facilities will be located beneath the terrace.

The design and its setting in the landscape

The author of this architectural concept is convinced that the shape of this concrete building will be in complete harmony with the group of surrounding hills on which the Goetheanum is allowed to stand. When creating the wooden structure of the earlier building the architect was not yet as familiar with their shapes as he is now, having come to know and love them during the course of more than a decade. The spirit of the surrounding countryside has therefore also been incorporated into the building in a way not possible eleven years ago.

(The rear of the building is to be modified in accordance with wishes expressed by Dornach parish council and the Solothurn government; this is not yet shown in the picture.)

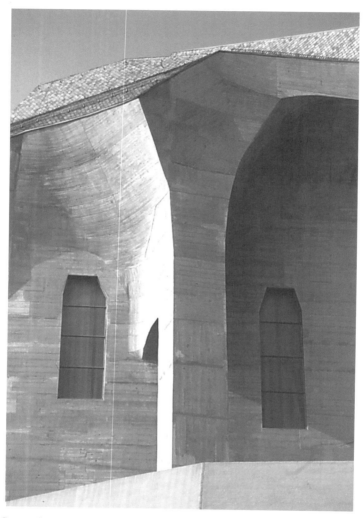

Second Goetheanum, detail of south elevation

Notes

GA = *Gesamtausgabe*, the collected works of Rudolf Steiner in the original German, published by Rudolf Steiner Verlag, Dornach, Switzerland.

Introduction

1. T. Benton *Art Nouveau Architecture*, Academy Editions, London.
2. W. Morris *Collected Works XXII*, p. 315.
3. N. Turgenieff-Pozzo *Zwölf Jahre der Arbeit am Goetheanum, 1913–1925*.
4. See R. Steiner *Bilder okkulter Siegel und Säulen. Der Münchener Kongress Pfingsten 1907 und seine Auswirkungen* (Occult seals and columns. The Munich Congress, Whitsun 1907, and its consequences) (GA 184), Dornach 1977.
5. See the chapter 'Das Goetheanum in seinen zehn Jahren' in R. Steiner *Der Goetheanumgedanke inmitten der Kulturkrisis der Gegenwart. Gesammelte Aufsätze aus der Wochenschrift 'Das Goetheanum' 1921–1925* (The concept of the Goetheanum in the midst of the present cultural crisis) (GA 36), Dornach 1961.
6. T. Cooper RIBA, 'Impressions of the Great Hall of the Goetheanum coming into being' *Newsletter, Art Section of the School of Spiritual Science*, Issue 9, Advent 1997.

PART I: AND THE TEMPLE IS THE HUMAN BEING
Lecture One (pages 3–21)

1. This lecture was given on the occasion of the first General Meeting of the Building Association (initially known as *Johannesbau Verein* and later *Goetheanum Verein*). This Association had been founded in April 1911 to promote, finance and manage the erection of the 'Johannesbau' in Munich. It continued in this role after the move to Dornach, seeing through the erection of both the first and second building. See Lecture Three, Note 1).
2. This refers to a lecture by Dr Ernst Wagner on 'Works of art as documents of human evolution' of which no record exists.
3. For the sequence of post-Atlantean cultural epochs see R. Steiner *Occult Science* (GA 13), Rudolf Steiner Press, London 1979.

4. The term 'Akashic Record' stems from ancient oriental tradition. It denotes the World Memory, a spiritual essence that retains traces of everything that has ever been accomplished in the world by conscious beings. See R. Steiner *Cosmic Memory* (GA 11), Harper & Row, New York 1981.

5. In his copy of Hegel's *Vorlesungen über Aesthetik* (Lectures on Aesthetics), Berlin 1835, Part 2, Chapter 1 'Unconscious Symbolism', Steiner underlined the following passage in Paragraph 1: 'Therefore, in their mysterious symbolism the works of Egyptian art are enigmas; they are an objective enigma as such. And the sphinx may be described as the symbol of what the Egyptian spirit really means. It is like the symbol of symbolism itself.'

6. See R. Steiner *The Influence of Spiritual Beings upon Man* (GA 102), Anthroposophic Press, New York 1982, lecture of 11 June 1908, and *Universe, Earth and Man* (GA 105), Rudolf Steiner Press, London 1987, lecture of 4 August 1908.

7. Two sentences from the German have been omitted in the English text: 'It would be hard to imagine a more suitable name than that chosen later by instinct [in the German language] for the Christian temple: "Dom" [cathedral]. This expresses a crowding together of human beings, a togetherness of people. "Dom" is intimately connected with [the ending] "tum", which expresses the same thing when used, for example, as the second syllable in the word "Volkstum" [nationality, national character, "peopleness"].'

8. See R. Steiner *The Temple Legend* (GA 93), Rudolf Steiner Press, London 1997.

9. Herodotus (c. 484-430 BC) first Greek historian, who travelled widely in Asia, Egypt and elsewhere. The construction of the Temple of Solomon is thought to have been planned in the years 959-952 BC. A temple in Jerusalem was destroyed by Nebuchadnezzar in 586 BC, so it would not have been standing at the time of Herodotus.

10. In 1909, 1910 and 1911 Steiner had given four lectures on each of these subjects. See *The Wisdom of Man, of the Soul and of the Spirit. Anthroposophy, Psychosophy, Pneumatosophy* (GA 115), Anthroposophic Press, New York 1971.

11. See R. Steiner *Bilder okkulter Siegel und Säulen*, op. cit. The lecture of 15 October 1911 ('The Stuttgart Building') is available in English in typescript at Rudolf Steiner Library, London. In it Steiner spoke about the difference between opaque and translucent paints on the walls.

12. Heinrich von Ferstel (1828–1883), professor of architecture and rector of the Technical University in Vienna. (See Part II, lecture 1, Note 2.)

13. *The Seven Wise Masters*, a cycle of stories of oriental origin translated into many European languages during the Middle Ages.

14. See R. Steiner *Turning Points in Spiritual History* (in GA 60), Spiritual Science Library, Blauvelt 1987, lecture of 9 March 1911.
15. See R. Steiner *Occult Science, an Outline*, op. cit.
16. The hierarchies referred to are the nine hierarchies of the angelic hosts described by Dionysus the Areopagite, of which the highest are the Seraphim and the lowest the angels.
17. The seven bodies are: physical, etheric, astral, ego, spirit self, life spirit and spirit man. See R. Steiner *Art in the Light of Mystery Wisdom* (GA 275), Rudolf Steiner Press, London 1996; and *Theosophy* (GA 9), Anthroposophic Press, Hudson 1994.

Lecture Two (pages 22–34)

1. The last general meeting of the German Section of the Theosophical Society took place in Berlin in December 1911. A year later the German Section was re-founded as the Anthroposophical Society. This lecture, given on 5 February 1913, took place early in the first general meeting of this new Society.
2. See Lecture One, Note 1.
3. See Lecture One, Note 4 on the Akashic Record.
4. R. Steiner *Theosophy*, op. cit.
5. Adolf Arenson (1855–1936), one of the leading active members of the Society in Stuttgart. He had given a lecture on 3 February 1913 on 'Studying spiritual science'.
6. See Lecture One, Note 11.
7. R. Steiner *The Portal of Initiation* (GA 14), Mystery Drama, translated by A. Bittleston, Rudolf Steiner Press, London 1982, Scene 8.
8. In February 1913 it was decided to abandon the Munich site and the project was moved to Dornach, near Basle, on an open country location in the foothills of the Jura mountains. The foundation stone was laid by Steiner on 20 September 1913.

Lecture Three (pages 35–49)

1. The building at Dornach was at first known as 'Johannesbau' after one of the main characters, Johannes Thomasius, in Steiner's Mystery Drama *The Portal of Initiation*. The name was still in use for this lecture, but for the purposes of this translation the designation 'Goetheanum' has been used. (Tr.)
2. Emil Grosheintz (1867–1946), dentist in Basle, prominent member of the Anthroposophical Society, who placed a parcel of land he owned at Dornach at the disposal of the building project, and became deputy chairman and subsequently chairman of the Building Association.
3. Known as the Glass House, this building still exists.

4. Thaddeus Rychter was the artist responsible for the interpretation and execution of Steiner's sketches for the engraved coloured glass windows. Eight lit the auditorium and one the entrance vestibule in the west. Rychter was called up in the First World War and subsequently lived in Jerusalem, where he died at the beginning of the Second World War.

5. The new art of movement in space developed in accordance with indications given by Steiner. See *An Introduction to Eurythmy* (in GA 277a), Anthroposophic Press, New York 1984.

6. Lecture One, Note 12.

7. This house (subsequently known as 'Rudolf Steiner Halde') had been the country residence of the Grosheintz family. It was acquired in 1921 and remodelled and extended by Steiner in 1923. See Erich Zimmer *Rudolf Steiner als Architekt von Wohn- und Zweckbauten* (Rudolf Steiner as a designer of buildings for domestic and other purposes), Stuttgart 1971.

8. The tasks of this association were taken over by the 'Goetheanum Association' at Christmas 1923.

9. Steiner later participated in the design of eight dwellings in the vicinity of the Goetheanum building, all of which can still be seen today. See Erich Zimmer *Rudolf Steiner als Architekt von Wohn- und Zweckbauten*, op. cit.

10. This General Meeting of the Anthroposophical Society was taking place in what was known as the 'Architektenhaus' in Berlin, where rooms could be hired for such occasions.

PART II: WAYS TO A NEW STYLE OF ARCHITECTURE

The diagrams in the text are sketches made during the lectures. (See Credits on p. vi.)

Lecture One (pages 53–77)

1. The construction of the first Goetheanum was financed entirely by donations; and the wood carving, painting and glass engraving work was largely voluntary.

2. Theophil Hansen (1813–1891), Danish architect. Having initially favoured early medieval styles he later became the main representative of Neo-Classicism. Architect of the Parliament and other buildings in Vienna.

Friedrich von Schmidt (1825–1891), German architect. As the main representative of the Neo-Gothic style he designed the Town Hall as well as other buildings in Vienna.

Heinrich von Ferstel (1828–1883), professor at the Vienna Polytechnic, designed the *Votivkirche*, the National Bank, the Austrian Museum for Art and Industry and the University in Italian Renaissance style.

Gottfried Semper (1803–1879), German architect who designed buildings in Dresden, Zürich and Vienna, including the 'Burgtheater' there. Main written work: *Der Stil in den technischen und tektonischen Künsten* (Style in the technical and tectonic arts), Frankfurt 1860/1863.

3. Joseph Bayer (1827–1910), professor of aesthetics at the Technical University of Vienna from 1871 to 1898. Main written work: *Aesthetik in Umrissen* (Aesthetics; an outline), 2 vols. Prague 1863. On his work see also *Die Technische Hochschule in Wien 1815 bis 1915* by Prof Dr Joseph Neuwirth, Vienna 1915.

4. Charles Darwin (1809–1882). Major works include *The Origin of Species* (1859) and *The Descent of Man* (1871).

5. Vitruvius Pollio, Roman architect and engineer under Julius Caesar and Augustus. Between 16 and 13 BC he wrote *De architectura* based on his own experience as well as on theoretical works by famous Greek architects.

   The anecdote as recounted by Vitruvius: It is told that the invention of this kind of capital came about as follows. The young daughter of a citizen of Corinth fell sick and died. After her funeral her nurse gathered up her toys in a basket which she placed on the grave, covering it with a roof tile so that the things would last longer out in the open. The basket happened to be resting on the root of an acanthus plant. When spring came the plant sent out leaves and stalks that curled their way round the outside of the basket which was still pressed down by the roof tile. Callimachos, the sculptor, happened to notice this interesting combination and used it as a model when designing capitals and other elements of buildings using what came to be known as the Corinthian Order.

6. The post-Atlantean epochs: third epoch 2906 to 747 BC; fourth epoch 747 BC to AD 1412. See also Part I, lecture 1, Note 3.

7. Part I, Lecture One, Note 4.

8. This alternation of earth and sun motifs, represented by plants borne in procession and described by Steiner as a finding of spiritual scientific research, has since been discovered in the design on an early Greek vase which is shown schematically below:

9. During a scientific discussion on 29 December 1922, published by the Section for Mathematics and Astronomy at the Goetheanum, Dornach, in *Mathematische Sendungen* No.6 (1930), Steiner described sunlight as being less than heavy, meaning that light shining downwards is actually a force pulling upwards.

   From another angle Steiner discussed the formative power of these two motifs as light and gravity in *Rosicrucianism and Modern Initiation* (GA 233a), Rudolf Steiner Press, London 1982. Here light is depicted by a triangle pointing downwards and gravity by one pointing upwards. Their interaction results in the hexagram, 'Solomon's key' to the world of form.

   Indications of this kind, arising from spiritual science, can throw light on shape and form in nature and art, on the styles of different cultures and on the element of composition as such.

10. Atlas, one of the Titans in Greek mythology, is represented in works of art as carrying the heavens or the terrestrial globe on his shoulders. The plural form 'Atlantes' is the classical term in architecture for male sculpted figures supporting a superstructure.

11. The strictly formalized character of the painted palm motif as seen, for example, in the archaeological department of the Acropolis Museum in Athens, is retained during the transition to relief. Here the palm motif is only chiselled into the stone in outline and is not raised up at all. This can be seen in the Erechtheum temple in Athens and also at Delphi. The original palm motif is only gradually metamorphosed into the much more naturalistic so-called acanthus leaf with the advent of the Corinthian capital.

   On the acanthus leaf see also F. Kempter *Akanthus—Die Entstehung eines Ornamentmotivs* (Acanthus—the birth of an ornamental motif), Leipzig, Strassburg, Zürich, 1934.

12. Steiner is here particularly referring to the interior of the hall and stage of the Goetheanum as it was envisaged for Munich. An illustration can be seen on p.18 in *The Goetheanum. Rudolf Steiner's Architectural Impulse*, Rudolf Steiner Press, London 1979.

13. Alois Riegl (1858–1905), Austrian art historian. His book *Stilfragen—Grundlegungen zu einer Geschichte der Ornamentik* (Questions of style—foundation for a history of ornamentation) appeared in Berlin in 1893. In it he said: 'I hope to be able to convince at least some of my colleagues that the acanthus is not the result of direct imitation of nature but arose out of an entirely artistic evolutionary process in the history of ornamentation.'

14. A marble portrait bust of a Roman noblewoman that was originally

thought to depict Clytie, a nymph turned into a flower for love of Apollo. Townley Collection, British Museum, London.

15. The architraves were 3 to 5 metres high and were made up of laminated boards 3 to 5 cm thick, cold glued together. This resulted in huge volumes of wood, and at first, in preparation for carving, workmen were asked to chop off the surplus parts with axes. A number of artists, however, preferred to work towards the desired forms from the start with chisels, going on to do the finer work with the gouge, and Steiner is agreeing to this here. Repeatedly he requested the artists to put warmth and sensitivity into the doubly curved surfaces in order to make their forms expressive so that they could become 'manifestations of life' and 'manifestations of consciousness'.

16. Adolf von Hildebrand (1847–1921), German sculptor. Wrote *Das Problem der Form in der bildenden Kunst* (The question of form in the visual arts), Strassburg 1913.

17. Beginning at the entrance to the auditorium of the First Goetheanum, the first pair of columns together with the section of the architrave between them were made of hornbeam, the second of ash, the third of cherry, the fourth of oak, the fifth of elm, the sixth of maple, and the seventh of birch. In the stage area beneath the smaller cupola the columns were made of two woods. Beginning at the junction with the auditorium the first pair was birch outside and maple inside, the second maple outside and elm inside, the third elm outside and oak inside, the fourth oak outside and cherry inside, the fifth cherry outside and ash inside, the sixth ash outside and hornbeam inside. The large sculpture in elm, known as 'The Representative of Humanity', was to have been positioned between the two sixth columns in the east beneath a canopy also in ash. The exterior of the building was in American oak, and the vestibule in the west in copper beech. For acoustic reasons the two cupolas were lined with plywood panels, then cork, finished with a layer of papier mâché with a white ground on which the paintings were executed.

18. Architectural symmetry—as opposed to sculptural symmetry in capitals—which refers to the right and left of the central axis in earlier architectural styles, is bound in a purely abstract mathematical sense to one line. Moreover, buildings in which, for example, the arches lying to the right and left of a column are placed symmetrically to one another, can also not be considered to have only a single axis of symmetry. This is different in the Goetheanum where a single axis of symmetry did indeed arise in a truly artistic sense out of the transformation by metamorphosis of the forms on the right and

left. This is an entirely new architectural element. This 'progression of the columns from the simplest capital and pedestal forms to the most complex ones in the middle, followed by a return to more simple forms, that is, the resolving of symmetry on all sides into a process of evolutionary metamorphosis' (lecture of 16 October 1920 in *Der Baugedanke von Dornach*, Dornach 1942) was begun by Steiner in the preparation of the congress hall in Munich at Whitsun 1907. Out of this arose the ellipsoid model building in Malsch (1909) and the domed hall in the first *Zweig* house in Stuttgart (1911). See *Bilder okkulter Siegel und Säulen*, op. cit. This conception was fully realized in the double-domed First Goetheanum in Dornach which was executed entirely in wood. Construction commenced in 1913, and on the night of New Year's Eve 1922/23 the building was burnt down to its concrete substructure. In the auditorium of the Second Goetheanum constructed in concrete—also designed by Steiner—the same concept of progressive evolution can now be seen in the trapezium-shaped plan of the auditorium opening out towards the stage designed by Christian Hitsch.
19. Identity unknown.
20. R. Steiner *The Portal of Initiation*, op. cit.
21. Auguste François Rodin (1840–1917), French sculptor.

Lecture Two (pages 78–98)

1. This lecture was given on the occasion of the dedication of the Glass House.
2. Part I, Lecture Three, Note 4.
3. See the lecture of 11 June 1908 in *The Influence of Spiritual Beings upon Man*, op. cit., given during the time when the model building in Malsch was being erected.
4. The fourth post-Atlantean epoch lasted from 745 BC to AD 1415. For the sequence of post-Atlantean cultural epochs and the development of individual human consciousness out of the group ego see R. Steiner *Occult Science*, op. cit.
5. The quotation is from Adolf von Hildebrand *Das Problem der Form in der bildenden Kunst*, op. cit. (See previous lecture, Note 16.)
6. See lecture given on 26 July 1914 (Part II, Lecture Five in this volume). Also R. Steiner *Colour* (GA 291), Rudolf Steiner Press, Sussex 1992.
7. In places where bends in the form made the surface concave, Steiner enhanced the surfaces by carving a further indentation

between them where the bend was most pronounced. An example of this may be seen in the two lower curvatures of the first section of the architrave in the west above the Saturn columns.

8. With the engraved designs in the glass windows Steiner inaugurated not only a new glass engraving technique but also a new kind of coloured glass window. The studio was built especially for the engraving of the coloured glass, and the expensive 5-millimetre thick panes were ordered before anyone knew precisely how the work might be tackled. The only thing to go on was Steiner's indication that a picture in light would arise where the glass was thinned by engraving. After some experimentation the necessary installation was designed, incorporating spray cooling, mobile gantries for the artists, motors with fitted flexible shafts, and various natural carborundum discs obtained from America. Experts are astonished by the fact that artists in Dornach came to be engraving glass with the help of tools such as carborundum discs and flexible shafts that had only just come on to the market and were as yet virtually unknown in 1914. The flexible shaft not only allows the artist to engrave large surfaces; it also enables light to shine through the work from the outset, so that the artist can watch as the picture arises in chiaroscuro. This is a far cry from the ancient cameo-cutting technique followed by Bohemian glass cutters.

9. The word 'abyss' is the spiritual scientific expression for the experience of the inner threshold which must be crossed when passing from normal day consciousness to spiritual consciousness. See R. Steiner's Four Mystery Dramas, op. cit., and *The Secrets of the Threshold* (GA 147), Anthroposophic Press, New York 1987, lecture of 30 August 1913.

Lecture Three (pages 99–115)

1. See lecture given on 17 June 1914 (Part II, Lecture Two in this volume).
2. See R. Steiner *Occult Science*, op. cit.
3. A passage from Lecture One in R. Steiner *Practical Advice to Teachers* (GA 294), Rudolf Steiner Press, London 1976, is relevant: 'In drawing lessons, rather than asking children to copy something, we should teach them how to draw primeval forms such as various angles, a circle, a spiral. Our point of departure will be the form itself rather than whether it is a copy of something else. We shall try to interest them in the form itself. You may remember the lecture in which I endeavoured to awaken an understanding for the origin of

the acanthus leaf motif by showing that the legend about the acanthus leaf being copied was quite false. The acanthus leaf motif arose out of an inner creativity and only subsequently was it felt to resemble the natural leaf. In drawing and painting we should take this into account. If we succeed, we shall help to put an end to the dreadful habit people have of thinking of works of art in terms of whether they are natural or not natural. It is irrelevant to say whether something has been correctly copied or not. Any resemblance with the external world is secondary. The important thing is that the person should be inwardly connected with the form itself. Even when drawing a nose you should be inwardly connected with the shape of that nose to the extent that you can only tell later on whether it is a good likeness or not.'

4. To facilitate individual work on these curves, their constructions are here described in brief.

Ellipse: Choose two points (foci) F and F', then somewhere alongside them draw a straight line SS' which is longer than the distance FF'. On SS' choose a first point 1. This point divides SS' into two portions, 1 and 1'. Using the compasses in the first portion, an arc is constructed around F, in the second around F'. The points of intersection of the two arcs are the first two points 1 of the ellipse. In the same way, from further points 2, 3, 4,... of the line SS', further pairs of portions arise: 2 and 2', 3 and 3', 4 and 4', and thus further points 2, 3, 4,... of the ellipse.

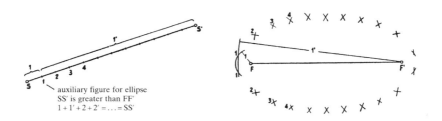

auxiliary figure for ellipse
SS' is greater than FF'
1 + 1' + 2 + 2' = ... = SS'

The construction of hyperbola, Cassini curve and division circle is similar to that of the ellipse. In each case there are two distances like 1 and 1', 2 and 2', etc, and for each portion an arc for F and for F'. The points of the curve are the points of intersection of these arcs. For each curve a different auxiliary figure is required. This provides the pairs of correlating distances.

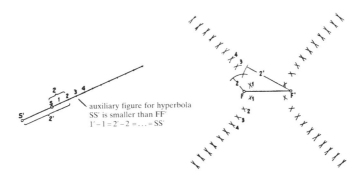

auxiliary figure for hyperbola
SS' is smaller than FF'
$1' - 1 = 2' - 2 = \ldots = SS'$

5. *Hyperbola*: Unlike the ellipse, the line SS' is smaller than FF', and the points 1, 2, 3, 4 ... lie on the *extension* of SS' instead of within it.

6. *Cassini curve*: Pairs of distances, which when multiplied together always give the same result, are determined, for example, with the aid of a circle (Centre M). The pairs of straight lines arise on the chords through a fixed point P within the circle. The arcs are drawn around F and F' with these distances and the Cassini curve results unless the measurements have been chosen so unfavourably that the arcs do not intersect. Random distances will, however, scarcely ever produce a *lemniscate*, since this has measurements which all coordinate exactly. The whole construction is best grasped by proceeding from the measurements of the lemniscate. It is then quite easy to see how the other forms arise from this:

As in the other cases, first choose the foci F and F'. Then draw a square anywhere whose sides equal the distance between the foci. The middle point of the square is M, and the middle point of a side is P. The circle through the corners of the square is then precisely the one that together with P leads to the lemniscate (Form II). A larger circle leads to the ellipse-like Form I, while a smaller one leads to Form III which consists of two correlating branches. Between I and II is the transitional form with the waist.

In the lecture given on 8 April 1911 at the International Congress of Philosophers in Bologna Steiner suggested these three forms of the Cassini curve as 'soul exercises':

'Mathematical figures can be of particular significance when they can be seen as symbols of universal processes. A good example is the curve of Cassini with its three shapes, the ellipse-like form, the lemniscate and the form comprising two correlating branches. What has to be achieved is the *feeling* engendered in the soul by the transition from one type of curve to another when it takes place in

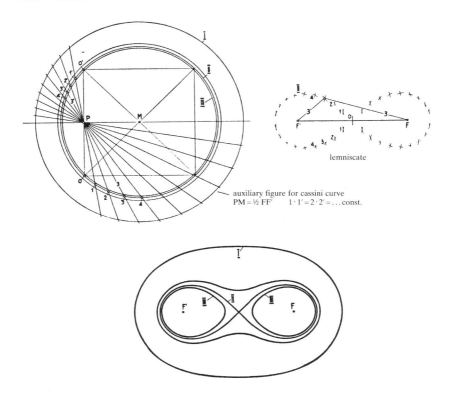

lemniscate

auxiliary figure for cassini curve
$PM = \frac{1}{2} FF'$ $1 \cdot 1' = 2 \cdot 2' = \dots$ const.

accordance with mathematical laws.' See R. Steiner *The Psychological Foundations of Anthroposophy* (GA 35), Anthroposophic Press, New York, and Rudolf Steiner Press, London.

7. *Division Circle*: [see diagram opposite] Pairs of distances which always yield the same quotient when divided are to be found on a pencil of rays with the apex S when it is intersected by two parallel lines. A favourable figure is arrived at if the distance between the parallel lines is the same as that between the foci and if S is presumed to be somewhere between the parallels.

8. The aspects of circle and sphere discussed in this lecture provide new criteria for the study of circular buildings in the different cultural epochs. Ancient Asiatic peoples based their round buildings on assumptions that differed greatly from those of the Romans; and Christian circular buildings—even though they may to some extent incorporate earlier forms—are intended to express quite different spiritual contents. See R. Steiner *Ideas for a New Europe* (in GA 194), Rudolf Steiner Press, Sussex 1992, lecture of 13 December 1919 mentioning the Grail temple. On Greco-Latin circular buildings see

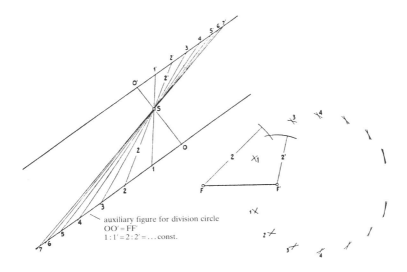

auxiliary figure for division circle
OO' = FF'
1 : 1' = 2 : 2' = ... const.

also the lectures *Der Dornacher Bau als Wahrzeichen geschichtlichen Werdens und künstlerischer Umwandlungsimpulse* (GA 287), Dornach 1985 (in English: typescript 'The Building at Dornach, Stages in Historical Development and a New Impulse in Art' available at Rudolf Steiner Library, London). In addition to the historically known circular buildings of Asia and Europe, Steiner also mentioned an impulse that came from the north of Europe around the year 1000. In the lecture given on 30 March 1914 (see Appendix) he mentioned the contrast between the wooden buildings of the Norsemen and what he described as the luciferic and ahrimanic influence revealed in the pointed arches of the Islamic or Arabian style. He pointed to a direct link between these northern wooden buildings and what he was aiming at in the forms of the Goetheanum. In addition to some old Norwegian stave churches constructed on an octahedral plan, the stone churches on the Danish island of Bornholm in the Baltic might also be cited as examples of this Nordic circular building impulse. The Swedish explorer Olaus Rudbeck (seventeenth century) and another Swede, Johan Göstaf Hallman (eighteenth century), both describe round wooden churches.

9. On the basis of this lecture, Carl Kemper discovered many years after Steiner's death that the ground plan of the first Goetheanum contained intersecting circles based on the ratio 1:3. See Carl Kemper *Der Bau* (The Goetheanum), Stuttgart 1974.

10. Regarding a) the positioning of the human being in space; b) the relationship between the architectural forms of the Goetheanum and

the experience of the dimensions of space as impulses of feeling, will and thinking; and c) the further evolution of the human being as shown in the onward progress of the will revealed through the metamorphosis of the column and architrave motifs as they relate to the historical sequence of cultures, see: R. Steiner *Die Polarität von Dauer und Entwickelung im Menschenleben* (GA 184), Dornach 1983, and *Der Dornacher Bau als Wahrzeichen geschichtlichen Werdens und künstlerischer Umwandlungsimpulse* (GA 287), Dornach 1985 (The building in Dornach as a document of historical progress and impulses of artistic metamorphosis), op. cit. A note by Steiner (Archive No. 247, Rudolf Steiner Nachlassverwaltung, Dornach) on the nature of the Goetheanum with reference the lecture of 28 June 1914 says:

'At first, people need only *will* as they step from column to column. A *feeling* for life arises in the right way if they understand the columns.'

In the cupola—the soul
In the forms—the body

Will—going forwards
Feeling—rising up
Thinking—reaching a conclusion

Lecture Four (pages 116–131)

1. These two beings were depicted by Steiner in his sculpture 'The Representative of Man' intended for the Goetheanum. They express the contrasting gestures of expansion (Lucifer) and contraction (Ahriman), life and death, heat and cold etc.
2. In *Sprüche in Prosa. Zur Kunst* (Sayings in prose: On Art) Goethe says: 'Beauty [in art] is a manifestation of secret laws of nature that would have remained forever hidden had beauty not appeared.' In his very first lecture, *Goethe as the Founder of a New Science of Aesthetics*, Anthroposophical Publishing Company, London 1922, (in GA 271), given before the Vienna Goethe Society on 8 November 1888, Steiner dealt thoroughly with this Goethean concept. That lecture is the starting point for the new direction in art he inaugurated.
3. See lecture given on 7 June 1914 (Part II, Lecture One in the present volume).
4. See Part II, Lecture One, Note 4.
5. The lecture was given in the carpenters' workshop where elements of the first Goetheanum were made by cutting, machining, laminating and glueing prior to being assembled and carved.

6. See R. Steiner *Colour*, op. cit.
7. Part II, Lecture One, Note 16.
8. In western culture, the ego began to be born into the human intellectual soul from 743 BC and into the consciousness soul from AD 1413. The ego's birth into spirit-self will begin from AD 3573. See R. Steiner *Occult Science*, op. cit.
9. Goethe *Faust*, Part I, Study.
10. The fifth post-Atlantean epoch began in 1413, coinciding with the transition from the medieval world to the Renaissance and the birth of the ego within the consciousness soul. For the sequence of post-Atlantean epochs see R. Steiner *Occult Science*, op. cit.

Lecture Five (pages 132–148)

1. Herman Grimm (1828-1901), art historian and writer. Steiner was referring to his essay 'Secession' in *Fragmente, Vol.II* (Fragments), 2 volumes, 1900. The title of the essay refers to groups of artists, calling themselves 'Secessionists', who were seceding from the hide-bound 'Association of German Painters': 'The wonderful thing about Goethe, which people are only just beginning to realize, is the way he proves the unity of all intellectual, spiritual effort ... All creative activity is a unity. Goethe not only advocated this unity of all intellectual, spiritual endeavour but also demonstrated it in the very way he led his life. This will not be fully understood until about the year 2000. In this sense Goethe was the first secessionist. He was self-sufficient. He did not want to be compared with others and he competed with nobody. He recognized that, whatever he might do, any task to which he directed his energy also contained something else, something universal, spiritual in the highest sense, which, in his opinion, had to be his point of departure.'
2. Asmus Jakob Carstens (1754–1798), German draftsman. See Herman Grimm in his essay 'Secession', op. cit.
3. See R. Steiner *Kunstgeschichte als Abbild innerer geistiger Impulse* (GA 292), Dornach 1981, available in English in typescript under the title 'The History of Art' at Rudolf Steiner Library, London.
4. Part II, Lecture Four, Note 2.
5. See R. Steiner *Occult Science*, op. cit.
6. Ibid.
7. See R. Steiner *Theosophy*. op. cit.
8. The painter Hilde Boos-Hamburger wrote about this water-colour sketch: 'I took my own notes in shorthand during the lecture ... and made an exact copy of the drawing in black and white on which I noted the various shades. That same evening I painted the exercise in

water-colour as exactly as I could . . .' Plate 1a shows a re-working by Hilde Boos-Hamburger of her original painting.

9. At the time of this lecture the attacks came especially from theological quarters. See the article 'Was soll die Geisteswissenschaft und wie wird sie von ihren Gegnern behandelt?' (What is the purpose of spiritual science and how is it being treated by its opponents?) in *Philosophie und Anthroposophie* (GA 35) Dornach 1984.

10. These further lectures took place in October 1914. See *Der Dornacher Bau als Wahrzeichen geschichtlichen Werdens und künstlerischer Umwandlungsimpulse*, op. cit., and *Colour*, op. cit.

11. These words were spoken on 26 July 1914 during days of tremendous tension leading up to the outbreak of the First World War on 1 August 1914.

Appendix (pages 151–176)

1. This passage is taken from notes written down from memory by an unknown person after a lecture given by Steiner to members of the Anthroposophical Society.

2. The complete lecture is in R. Steiner *Vorstufen zum Mysterium von Golgatha* (GA 152), Dornach 1990.

3. See R. Steiner *The Christmas Conference for the Foundation of the General Anthroposophical Society 1923/24* (GA 260), Anthroposophic Press, New York 1990. (Morning, 31 December 1923.)

4. 'Haus Duldeck' is situated to the south-west of the Goetheanum and was designed and erected 1914-15.

5. 'Rudolf Steiner Halde', north-west wing, also known as the 'Eurythmeum', which was designed by Steiner and erected in 1923 as an extension to the older building.

6. It is clear that Steiner considered the terrace level as the ground floor with a lower ground floor below within the podium. In the old Goetheanum there was only one floor at the terrace level with an entrance into the auditorium from the west. In the new Goetheanum this west entrance to the auditorium was to be raised a full floor so that a new floor could be inserted at terrace level.

7. See R. Steiner *An Introduction to Eurythmy*, op. cit.

8. See R. Steiner 'The Envy of the Gods—The Envy of Human Beings' in *The Christmas Conference*, op. cit. (Evening, 31 December 1923.)

9. See R. Steiner *The Christmas Conference*, op. cit. (Morning, 1 January 1924.)